**180 Devotions
and Worship
Activities for
Preschoolers**

Little Hearts for Jesus

Devotional

SALLY PIERSON DILLON

ʀ

REVIEW AND HERALD® PUBLISHING ASSOCIATION

Since 1861 | www.reviewandherald.com

Credits

Copyright © 1999 by
Review and Herald® Publishing Association
International copyright secured

The author assumes full responsibility for the
accuracy of all facts and quotations as cited
in this book.

This book was
Edited by Jeannette R. Johnson
Copyedited by James Cavil
Designed by Patricia S. Wegh
Illustrations by Mary Bausman
Electronic make-up by Shirley M. Bolivar
Typeset: 11/13 New Century Schoolbook

BOOKS BY SALLY PIERSON DILLON

War of the Ages series
Hugs From Jesus

To order, call **1-800-765-6955.**

Printed by Pacific Press® Publishing Association
PRINTED IN U.S.A.

Library of Congress Cataloging Data
Dillon Sally Pierson, 1959-2007.
 Little hearts for Jesus : devotional / Sally Pierson
Dillon.
   1 v. (unpaged)—(180 devotions and worship activi-
ties for preschoolers)
 ISBN 978-0-8280-1344-4
1. Bible stories, English.—O.T. Study and teaching
(Preschool). 2. Preschool children—Prayers and de-
votions.
3. Seventh-day Adventists—Prayers and devotions.
I. Title.
 BS546 .D55 1999
 242/.62 21

                                    00687764

May 2018

My Little Devotional

_____

Dedication

To Don and Betty Pierson (my parents),
who instilled in me a love for family worship
from as long ago as I remember;

To Don and Mike (my sons), without whom these
activities would never have been developed;

To Bruce (my husband), without whom Don and Mike would
have never been, and without whose encouragement this
book might never have been written.

Contents

Contents

Contents

Contents

Contents

Contents

Contents

Contents

Contents

Contents

Contents

Contents

Contents

Contents

Contents

Dear Mom and Dad...

The Bible gives us counsel on how to teach God's Word to our children in Deuteronomy 6:6, 7. **"These commandments that I give you today are to be upon your hearts. Impress them on your children. Talk about them when you sit at home and when you walk along the road, when you lie down and when you get up" (NIV).**

These devotions for preschoolers include devotions appropriate for different times in the family schedule: devotions for mealtimes, bath time and bedtime; devotions for laundry day and for outdoors. And, of course, devotions for any time.

A wise person once said, If there were more mothers like Mary, there would be more children like Jesus. Mary taught Jesus from the Scriptures, from nature, from God's providence. These devotions are designed to give you these tools. There are devotions based on Bible stories (the Scriptures), nature, and God's gifts to us (His providence). There are also devotions on caring for their bodies and forming good health habits, and some miscellaneous worship devotions.

Preschoolers find it hard to sit still and be read to, especially without pictures. This devotional is not for reading—it is for doing. Besides, we remember only 10 percent of what we hear, but 90 percent of what we *do.*

Preschoolers are fond of repetition. They choose a favorite story and want it repeated again and again. You will find some stories repeated in this manuscript with different activities accompanying them, and repeated activities with different stories. This satisfies the preschooler's need for repetition without causing terminal boredom to the rest of the family!

Most of these devotions can be adapted to any preschooler. Every child is different, so adapt any devotions to appeal to your child at his or her level of understanding.

Often it is difficult to have on hand

the exact craft items called for in an activity. The index grid should help you with your planning and shopping. Materials are divided as follows: your child's own toys, household items, stationery items, craft items.

Your child's own toys include: stuffed animals, blocks, plastic animals, lizards, frogs, and bugs. Also needed is a good nature book with pictures of animals, birds, fish, insects, reptiles, and sea animals.

Household items include: laundry baskets, towels, blankets, dishes, paper plates and cups, newspaper, cookie cutters, cotton balls, cinnamon, food coloring, Band-aids, and sponges, as well as dish soap and common food items, such as dried beans, macaroni, etc.

Stationery items include: old magazines for cutting up, scissors, construction paper, glue, stapler, pencils, both washable and permanent markers, clear tape, paper clips, and crayons.

Craft items to keep on hand include: nature stickers, pipe cleaners, a box of Popsicle sticks, and colored yarns (including green).

Prayer should always be a part of devotions. Have your preschooler repeat a short prayer after you following each devotional activity. Often a single-sentence prayer is included at the end of a devotional to help you.

By using activity devotions you will equip your child for ministry. The activities are fun, and you will often hear them being repeated with your child's friends who come over to play. Nobody is ever too young to witness!

Don't feel limited to using these devotions as they are written. Be creative; adapt; play. Getting to know God should be fun. Enjoy!

—SALLY PIERSON DILLON

Dear Parents

Joshua and Jericho

Materials: *blocks, toy horns*

Jericho was a city with a big wall around it. *[Use blocks to build wall as you talk.]* The people felt safe inside, but they didn't love God and didn't like the people who did.

God's people came to the city of Jericho. Joshua (their leader) asked God what they should do. God told them to walk around the city quietly every day for seven days.

[March with your child around the block city.] The people inside Jericho thought that was a silly way of attacking it! But God's people did exactly what God told them to do.

On the seventh day they marched around just as they had done every day. But when they got all the way around, instead of going home they marched around again. *[Continue to march with child.]*

When they had marched around seven times, they stopped. Then God's priests blew their horns, and all the people shouted as loudly as they could. *[Blow horns or shout loudly.]* Suddenly the walls started to crumble. *[Start to push block walls over.]* God is stronger than anything! Even big city walls! Hooray for God! *[Clap and cheer loudly.]*

Theme: God's Word

Storm at Sea

Materials: *laundry basket*

esus was tired. He and His friends decided to go across the lake in a boat. *[Place your child in laundry basket.]* The boat rocked gently. *[Rock basket gently.]* Jesus went to sleep.

Soon the wind began to blow. *[Have child make wind noises.]* It began to rain. *[Sprinkle drops of water on child.]* Soon, there was even thunder and lightning! *[Make loud thunder noises.]* The boat tossed back and forth. *[Rock basket more vigorously.]*

Jesus' friends were afraid. Should they ask Jesus for help? *[It is always good to ask Jesus for help when you have a problem.]*

Jesus always hears when His friends ask Him for help. He stood up and put His arms out. *[Have child stand up and stretch arms out.]* He told the storm to be quiet! *[Have child tell storm to be quiet.]* Suddenly the storm stopped. *[Rock basket gently again.]*

Jesus made the water and the wind, so He could tell them what to do.

Dear God, help me remember not to be afraid during storms, since You made the wind and the rain and can tell them what to do. Amen.

Theme: God's Word

#2

Baby Moses

Materials: *laundry basket, blanket (optional)*

B aby Moses' mother loved him. She kissed the top of his little head. *[Kiss child's head.]* His daddy loved him. He hugged him tightly. *[Hug child.]* Big brother Aaron and big sister Miriam loved him too.

But the mean king where Baby Moses lived did not love him. He made a law that all the baby boys who were born to the families of God's people should be thrown into the river!

Mother wrapped Baby Moses in a blanket. *[Wrap child in blanket.]* She placed him in a special basket. *[Place wrapped child in basket.]* She put it among the tall river reeds to keep it from floating away. Mother asked God to watch over her baby and keep him safe.

The king's daughter saw the basket. *[Peek into the basket.]* "Oh, what a cute baby!" she said. This would be her very own baby. The king would not throw him back into the river. She got Moses' very own mother to be his baby-sitter. His mother was so happy to have Baby Moses home. *[Lift child out of basket and hug.]*

#3

Theme: God's Word

Noah

Materials: *laundry basket, miscellaneous stuffed animals*

oah loved God. The people where he lived did not love God. They were mean and did bad things. One day God told Noah there would be a big flood. He told Noah to build a big boat. Then all the people who wanted to be safe could go inside the boat. They would float on top of the water and be safe from the flood. Noah built the boat, just as God told him to. *[Place laundry basket on the floor in front of child.]*

Noah told all the people what God had said. Mrs. Noah believed him. So did Noah's sons and their wives. The people laughed and made fun of him. *[Point and laugh.]*

One day a very strange thing happened. Animals started coming to the boat from all over the earth. *[Have child bring animals and put them in the basket.]* Noah had lots and lots of animals in his boat. Then Noah and his family got in too. *[Have child climb into basket with animals.]* When the flood came, God took good care of Noah's family and the animals.

Dear God, You took good care of Noah and the animals. Please take good care of me, too. Amen.

Theme: God's Word

#4

Joseph's Pretty Coat

Materials: *large white T-shirt (Daddy's will be fine), newspaper, water-soluble markers*

The Bible tells us a story about a boy named Joseph. Joseph's daddy loved him very much. *[Hug child.]* He decided to make Joseph a special robe. *[Place newspaper on table. Lay T-shirt on table and insert folded newspaper inside shirt so colors won't bleed through.]*

Joseph's dad didn't want to give him a plain robe. He wanted to make it lots of different colors! *[Hold markers in front of child.]* What color did he choose first? Draw a long stripe on the T-shirt. What color do you think he chose next? *[Have child help*

color stripes on T-shirt. When you're finished, or child's interest is waning, stop. It doesn't have to be solid stripes!]

Then Joseph's daddy let Joseph put the pretty robe on and wear it. *[Slip the T-shirt over the child's head and let the child wear the "robe" as long as he / she is interested. Then throw it in the laundry. Water-soluble ink will wash out, and you can do it again another day!]*

Dear God, You made sure Joseph's dad had clothes for him. Thank You for making sure I have clothes to wear too. Amen.

Theme: God's Word

#5

Tail Talk

Materials: *kitten and puppy [use pictures or stuffed animals if real pets are unavailable]*

When a dog wags its tail, it is saying it is happy. Can you pet a dog with a wagging tail? Yes, if you know it. (We don't pet animals we don't know.) *[Have child pet dog/stuffed dog/picture.]*

When a cat wags its tail, it means trouble! If you tried to pet a cat whose tail was wagging you could end up getting scratched—or even having a cat bite. *Ouch!*

I'm going to pretend I am a dog, and you see if it is safe to pet me. I'm going to use my arm for a tail (since I don't have a tail). *[Wag arm. When child pets you, act happy.]* Now what about this dog? *[Make your arm straight and hang down. If child tries to pet you now, growl and bark.]* Now *you* be the dog.

[Repeat process, pretending to be a cat.]

Aren't you glad Jesus made a way for dogs and cats to tell us how they are feeling? He did that because He didn't want to see us get scratched or bitten.

You can talk, so you don't need a tail to tell people how you are feeling. And even if you don't talk, Jesus knows just how you are feeling all the time. I'm so glad—you'd look funny with a tail!

Theme: Nature

Creation: Day 5, Part 1

Materials: *paper plates (Chinette or styrofoam, with a flat-lip edge), glue, Goldfish crackers, white glue, blue or green plastic film wrap. Optional: yarn (for seaweed), sea animal stickers, small seashells or small pasta shells*

In the beginning God made our world and everything in it. On the fifth day of His work He made all the sea animals. He made *[name the different creatures as you point to them; if you aren't using sea animal stickers, point to pictures of sea animals in a book].*

Let's make a picture of some things Jesus made on the fifth day. *[Help child by dotting glue on the backs of the yarn seaweed and fish crackers so child can glue them on the plate. When the undersea masterpiece is finished, use plastic wrap to cover* plate. Tape securely to the back. Now child's Undersea Aquarium is ready to display on child's wall or be shown around to friends. Make sure to have extra fish crackers—often more get eaten than put on the plate.]*

Theme: God's Word/Nature

Creation: Day 5, Part 2

Materials: *fish and sea animal cookie cutters; gelatin in several colors (including green), prepared one-inch thick in large flat pans; table (scrubbed clean enough to eat from!) or a very large platter*

U*se prepared flavored fruit gelatins, using only half the water called for in the recipe on the box. It makes gelatin firmer, easier to handle. After cutting out animal shapes with cookie cutters, scoop out animals with a pancake turner.]*

In the beginning God made our world and everything in it. On the fifth day of His work He made all the sea animals. *[Name each animal as you point to the cookie cutters. Use a round one for clams or crabs, and add licorice legs for an octopus.]*

God had already made the ocean where the sea animals would live. *[Cut long strips of green gelatin and lay on table for seaweed. Have child decide where to put each fish and animal as they are "created." Take a picture for the child's scrapbook.]*

The Bible says that when God was finished creating on the fifth day, He looked at everything He had made. He said, "It is good," and He didn't eat them. But we are going to! *[Enjoy eating the undersea masterpiece with child.]*

Dear God, Thank You for making sea animals. And thank You for making me. Amen.

Theme: God's Word/Nature

#8

Creation: Day 5, Part 3

Materials: *your imagination*

In the beginning God made our world and everything in it. On the fifth day of His work He made all the sea animals. He made all the birds, too. *[Look through a nature book at different sea creatures and birds, naming each one as you go.]*

Can you guess which sea creature (bird) I am? *[Mime creature for child. Help with clues if the child has difficulty guessing. Then have child mime with you, pretending to be that animal.]*

The Bible says that when God was fin-ished creating on the fifth day, He looked at everything He had made. He said, "It is good."

Theme: God's Word/Nature

Creation: Day 5, Part 4

Materials: *balsa glider (sold in most drug/dime stores)*

Have child help assemble glider. You can even decorate it with markers. Go to a place you can throw it off a little hill or cliff, if possible. Use a watch with a second hand to time how long glider can stay in the air.]

The glider we made stayed up in the air for [*say how many*] seconds. Now let's watch the birds fly. How many seconds can they stay up in the air? We can't really measure that, because God made the birds so they can stay in the air as long as they want to. Isn't God awesome?

Theme: God's Word/Nature

#10

Creation: Day 5, Part 5

Materials: *blue or green Jell-O, gummy fish or gummy sharks*

O n the fifth day of Creation God made the ocean and put all the fish and sea animals in it.

[Before worship, prepare the Jell-O and pour into small, clear glasses. Allow your child to fill each Jell-O "ocean" with gummy fish or sharks, then place in the refrigerator. Have a prayer thanking God for fish and sea animals before eating the Jell-O for a snack or dessert.]

#11

Theme: God's Word/Nature

Jesus and Mother Hens

Materials: *blanket*

pread blanket across your shoulders and grasp corners in each hand to simulate wings.] Today I am being a mama hen. A hen is a mother chicken. Chickens are birds, even though they don't fly very well. They use their wings for other things, though. Whenever there is a mean animal close by who might like a little chick for breakfast, the mama hen swoops over *[swoop over and wrap your child in your blanket-wings]* and scoops her little chick under her wings.

It feels all safe and snuggly and warm under mama hen's wings. Jesus once said that He wanted to snuggle us under His wings just like a mama hen snuggles her chicks. He cried because He knew there were many sad and dangerous things that would happen to people, and they wouldn't come to Him to be safe.

We can't see Jesus, but we can ask to snuggle under His wings and be safe. *[Wrap your blanket wings around your child again.]*

Theme: God's Word/Nature

#12

Devotion

The Lost Sheep

Materials: *bag of cotton balls*

H*ide several cotton balls around the room (in plain sight).]*
Jesus told a story in the Bible about a man who had 100 sheep. That is a *lot* of sheep! *[Look at a picture of sheep.]* Can you imagine having 100 of them that all belonged to you?

One day, when the sheep were all coming home to go to bed, the man noticed one sheep was missing. This meant that he still had 99 sheep. Did one missing sheep matter? It certainly did! He went out and looked and looked until he found his missing sheep.

Jesus loves us so much that even though He has many other people who love Him, if you got lost He would go looking and looking until He found you. That is because you are so important to Him.

See this fluffy cotton ball? Let's pretend this is a sheep. There are several lost sheep just like this one hidden in the room here. Can you find them? *[You may have to hide them again after your child finds them all. This was a favorite game at our house!]*

#13

Theme: God's Word

Sabbath Is Special

Materials: *pita bread, cinnamon, melted butter, sugar*

God made the Sabbath the same week that He created our world. He made it come every seventh day because He knew we needed a day to rest and be with Him. He wanted the Sabbath to be special for everybody.

Way back in Bible times showbread was a special Sabbath bread that the people who worked for God got to eat on Sabbath. Each week they baked the round flat loaves. *[Give child a pita.]* They would put olive oil on it. *[Use a pastry brush to apply melted butter, and let child do the same.]* Then they sprin-

kled it with special spices. *[Mix cinnamon and sugar in a small container and sprinkle on pitas.]*

They left these loaves on a golden table in God's house for a whole week. On Sabbath they brought new bread into God's house; then they could eat the ones they took out. *[Eat the pita breads with your child.]*

God thought of everything to make His day really special, even good things to eat!

Dear God, Thank You for making the Sabbath, and thank You for remembering that we like special things to eat. Amen.

Theme: God's Word

Devotion

#14

Why Ice Floats

Materials: *large bowl of water, several ice cubes, heavy plastic turtle or frog*

Have child drop ice cubes in bowl of water.] What happens? Can you make the ice stay on the bottom? Why not? Did you know that God makes ice float for a special reason?

[Have child place frog or turtle in the bottom of the bowl.] In cold weather some of the water on ponds turns to ice. The turtles and frogs hide at the bottom of the pond and sleep until warmer weather. If the ice was at the bottom of the pond, it would freeze the turtles. God made ice float so that the little creatures at the bottom of the pond would be safe in the winter.

Every time you have ice in your drinking glass, remember why ice floats and how good God is!

#15

Theme: Nature

Thank-You Book

Materials: *scrapbook (use any type—sketch book to loose-leaf version; needs room for lots of glued-in stuff), safety scissors, glue stick, or Scotch tape*

T*his devotion can be returned to again and again, being thankful for something different each time. Provide stickers and magazines, seed catalogs, and junk mail to cut pictures from. Paste in favorite pictures from coloring book. During the holiday season, cut up greeting cards and even photographs of siblings and friends.*

[On a "thankful day," allow the child to be in charge of worship. Go through the "thankful book" and thank God for each thing pictured.]

Theme: Thankfulness

Dear God, Thank You for _____. Amen.

#16

Jesus Made My Feet

Materials: *your bare feet; pictures of birds, cats, and horses (with the feet visible)*

Optional: *Draw around child's foot with a pen onto a page in their "thankful book" and write "My feet are just right" below it.*

Birds have strong, clawlike feet so they can hang on to branches. God knew just what kind of feet birds needed!

Cats have soft pads on the bottoms of their feet for sneaking around quietly. *[Try sneaking around barefoot.]* But a cat's feet have something your feet don't—sharp claws that can scratch if the cat needs protection. Then they fold back into the cat's paws so it can have soft, sneaky feet again.

Horses have different feet too. It almost looks as though God created horses with their shoes on! God knew exactly what kind of protection a horse's feet would need.

What about your feet? Do you have claws to hang on to tree branches with? (No; Jesus made you so you didn't have to live in trees!) Do you have pop-out claws like the cat has? (Jesus gave you parents to protect you, so you don't need claws!) Do you have hooves like the horse? (Jesus knew that when you needed to run on hard surfaces you could wear shoes!)

Your feet are different, but they are just right for you!

#17

Theme: Nature/Healthy Body

Jesus Made My Hands

Materials: *a pair of socks*

Aren't you glad Jesus gave us hands instead of just making soft little paws at the ends of our arms? *[Put socks over your child's hands. Put socks over your hands too.]*

Without your fingers, can you *[try each activity]*:

pick up your toys?
eat a cookie?
scratch your ear?
point to your mother?
color with your crayons?

It's hard, isn't it? Jesus knew we would want to do things that would be hard to do without fingers. I'm so glad Jesus is so smart and gave us just what we need!

Theme: Nature/Healthy Body

#18

Jesus Made My Arms

God gave birds wings. Can you fly? *[Have child flap his/her "wings."]* Why can't you? God didn't give you wings, did He?

God gave seals flippers. (They help the seal swim very fast.) People can swim by using their arms and legs, but they are never as fast as seals, because seals have flippers.

God gave dogs paws with claws. (They are good for digging in the dirt.) People can dig in the dirt too, but our fingernails are not as good for digging as a dog's claws are, so we sometimes use a shovel.

God gave calves long front legs. What are the calves' legs for? (Calves need to stand on all four of their legs because they can't keep their balance by standing up on two legs as you can.)

Little boys and girls like to give hugs. God knew you needed arms for that. Can a bird give hugs? Can a seal give hugs? Can a dog give hugs? Can calves give hugs? *[Hug your child.]*

I'm so glad God gave us arms so we could hug each other! God made everything and everyone just right!

Dear God, Thank You for giving me arms. Amen.

#19

Theme: Nature/Healthy Body

Plants Drink Water Too

Materials: *stalk of celery (or a white carnation), food coloring (blue or red)*

Did you know that in order to grow properly plants need to drink water, just like you do? Let's fix a glass of water for this piece of celery. We will color the water so we can see if the plant drinks any. *[Place stalk of celery in glass of colored water. It's fun to make a glass each of blue, red, and green. Always have one in a glass of clear water to compare to the colored ones.]*

Plants drink slowly, so we will need to let it drink all day, then check it after dinner tonight.

Later . . .
Look! The celery drank the colored water. See how the leaves are blue?

Theme: Nature

#20

Elijah

Materials: *large towel, slices of bread*

God talked to Elijah and told him He was not happy with King Ahab and his mean wife, Jezebel. They did not love God, and got the other people to worship idols instead of worshiping God. God was sad. God decided to show them that He was stronger than their idols by not sending any rain for three whole years.

King Ahab and Queen Jezebel did not like Elijah's message. They sent soldiers after Elijah to kill him. God told Elijah where to hide.

Elijah camped by a little brook. Every day the birds brought him food. The birds were working for God.

[Have child lay across the center of the towel with head and arms off the edge. Pick up the two ends of the towel and have the child flap his/her wings (arms) and fly over to get the bread (in their mouths, since birds don't have hands), and then fly over to Elijah's camp. Have child drop the bread for Elijah.]

Even birds can be God's helpers. Do you want to be God's helper too? Just tell Him.

Dear God, I would like to be Your helper too. Help me to find out how I can help. Amen.

Theme: God's Word

Elijah and Elisha

Materials: *large towel for a cape*

P ut towel over your shoulders as a cape.] Let's pretend I am Elijah and you are Elisha. Elijah talked to God, and God talked to him. Elijah knew he was not going to be a prophet much longer. He trained Elisha to be the next prophet so God would still have someone to talk to and tell people how He wanted them to live.

Elijah had been such a good one—Elisha hoped he could be as good. He asked God to give him twice as much of His Spirit as He had given Elijah.

God sent a fiery chariot to take Elijah to live with Him without ever dying. As Elijah was taken up into the sky, his cape fell down to Elisha.

[Gallop across the room as if being taken away in a chariot, then pull the "cape"off your shoulders and drop it on the child.]

Elisha knew God was giving him what he had asked for. He became a great prophet, just as God had planned.

If we ask for God's Spirit, God will give it to us, too. He may not drop a cape on us to let us know, but He sends it to us just the same.

Theme: God's Word

#22

Trees for Supper

Materials: *paper, crayons or markers*

Fold paper into a pleat so there's a hidden fold that can be unfolded by pulling paper out straight. Before worship, prepare several sheets of paper this way. In one pleat, draw a caterpillar eating a leaf.]

Did you know God made trees for supper? Not for *your* supper, except when the tree grows apples or other fruit you like to eat. But He made trees for some of His other creatures.

[Draw, or have child draw, a tree on the pleated paper over the pleat. Then have
child pull the paper flat so the pleat is open and the caterpillar having supper is visible.]

Surprise! The caterpillar is eating leaves for supper.

Let's draw another tree. *[You can allow child to add the surprise animal, or you can draw it in ahead of time. Other surprise animals can include bee and honey, worm in an apple, woodpecker on trunk.]*

God plans for everyone's supper. He makes sure you have good food for your supper, and He makes sure His creatures have supper too. God is so good!

Theme: Nature

Trees for Homes

Materials: *paper, crayons or markers*

F old paper into a pleat so there's a hidden fold that can be unfolded by pulling paper out straight. Before worship, prepare several sheets of paper this way. In one pleat, draw a nest with eggs.]

Did you know God made trees for houses? Not like your house, but houses for some of His other creatures.

[Draw, or have child draw, a tree on the pleated paper, over the pleat. Then let child pull the paper flat so the pleat is open and the bird's nest is visible.]

Surprise! The house is in the tree.

Let's draw another tree. *[The child can add the surprise animal, or you can draw it in ahead of time. Other surprise animals can include bee and honey, squirrel, raccoons, caterpillars.]*

God plans for everyone to have a home. He makes sure you have someplace safe and warm to live, and He makes sure His creatures have homes too. God is so good!

Theme: Nature

#24

Hatching Eggs, Part 1

Materials: *paper, crayons or markers*

Fold several sheets of paper into a pleat so there's a hidden fold that can be unfolded by pulling paper out straight. Draw a snake in one pleat.]

Lots of God's baby animals hatch from eggs.

[Help child draw an egg on one sheet of pleated paper, over the pleat. Then have child pull the paper flat so the pleat is open and the baby snake is visible.]

Surprise! God made a baby snake grow in this snake's egg.

Let's draw another egg. [Use stickers, allow child to add the surprise animal, or draw it in ahead of time. Other surprise animals can include a frog, a lizard, a bird, a baby chick, a baby turtle.]

God plans for all kinds of animals to have babies. Some hatch from eggs; some don't. You didn't hatch from an egg. You grew inside your mother. God made a special way for each animal to have babies. God is so good!

Dear God, thank You for making a way for each kind of animal to have babies. And thank You for making me. Amen.

Theme: Nature

Hatching Eggs, Part 2

Materials: *small plastic eggs (buy around Easter time, or use larger ones that come with panty hose), small plastic animals (snake, turtle, bird, lizard, frog, or any other animals that hatch from eggs; can fold up a picture of each if you don't have the animals you need).*

efore worship, hide the baby animals in the eggs.]*

Did you know that lots of God's baby animals hatch from eggs? They do!

[Allow child to open an egg.]

Surprise! God made a baby snake grow in this snake's egg.

Let's open another egg. *[After child has opened all the eggs, you may want to let him/her refill the eggs and open them again.]*

God plans all kinds of ways for animals to have babies. Some hatch from eggs. Some don't. You didn't hatch from an egg—you grew inside your mother. God made a special way for each animal to have babies. God is so good!

Theme: Nature

Jonah

Materials: *paper, crayons or markers*

Wold three sheets of paper into a pleat so there's a hidden fold. Draw a stick man in two of the pleated papers, and several stick characters, praying, in the third.]

God told Jonah to go to Nineveh to tell the bad people to change their ways or God would destroy their city. Jonah didn't want to do that, so he got on a boat and hid down inside. *[Draw a boat on pleated paper, over fold.]* Did God know where Jonah was hiding? *[Pull pleat open to reveal Jonah inside the boat.]* Yes, God knows where we are all the time!

God sent a big storm. The people on the boat threw Jonah into the ocean, and the storm stopped. God sent a big fish. *[Draw a big fish over pleat.]* The big fish swallowed Jonah. *[Pull pleat open to show Jonah in the fish.]*

Jonah promised God he would go to Nineveh. God made the fish spit Jonah out on the beach.

[Draw a walled city with a gate in the front.] The people in Nineveh listened to Jonah's message. *[Pull pleat open to show kneeling people.]* They asked God to forgive them. And He did.

#27

Theme: God's Word

Zacchaeus, Friend of Jesus

Materials: *paper, crayons or markers*

Fold paper into a pleat so there's a hidden fold that can be unfolded by pulling paper out straight. Draw a stick man in the pleat.]

One day Zacchaeus heard that Jesus was coming to his town. He wanted to see Jesus so badly. But he was afraid Jesus wouldn't like him, because a lot of people in his town didn't like him at all. A huge crowd of people gathered, all trying to see Jesus. Zacchaeus couldn't see over their heads. He was too short. He tried standing on his tiptoes. *[Have child stand on tiptoe.]* He tried jumping up as high as he could.

[Have child jump.] Finally he had an idea. He climbed up in a tree. Then he could see Jesus. *[Have child draw a tree on pleated paper.]*

Soon Jesus walked right by the tree. *[Draw stick figure next to tree.]* Did Jesus know Zacchaeus was in the tree? *[Open to show Zacchaeus hiding in tree.]* Jesus looked up and said, "Come down! I want to come to your house for supper!"

Zacchaeus was so surprised. Jesus liked him and wanted to be his friend!

Dear God, thank You for being friends with short people, too! Amen.

Theme: God's Word

#28

We Need Water

Materials: *bowl of water, blotting paper,
crayons (optional), scissors*

D*raw, or have child draw, flowers on
blotting paper. Flowers with five
individual petals are the easiest for
this activity. Color the flowers, if desired,
then cut them out. Fold the petals into the
center, and color the top green.]*

Flowers start out as a bud, like this
green one. If they don't get any water they
will dry up and turn brown and fall off the
plant. That isn't very pretty, is it?

They need water to grow and blossom
and be beautiful, as God intended them to
be. What happens when we put this bud in
the water? *[Place "bud," folded petal side
up, in water. Watch the flower magically
open. Repeat as many times as child de-
sires.]* God made flowers to be pretty, if they
get enough water.

You too need water to grow and be the
way God wants you to be. Let's go have a
drink of water!

#29

Theme: Nature

Red Worship

Materials: *large piece of paper or poster board, red crayon or marker*

Today we are going to have a red worship. We are going to think of all the red things we are thankful for. We will draw them on this piece of paper, and then we will thank Jesus for them.

[Allow child to draw, or draw and allow child to color items. This activity can work for any color.]

Dear God, thank You for making red things. Thank You for [name each item on paper]. *Amen.*

Theme: Thankfulness

LHFJ-7

#30

The Lost Coin

Materials: *Cheerios, Fruit Loops, or other "O"-shaped cereal and a shoelace or other short piece of string. Tie a large knot, or attach a bead or similar object on the end to keep the cereal on.*

Jesus once told a story about a woman who had saved 10 special coins she had received as a present when she got married. One day as she was cleaning her house she realized she had lost one of the special coins. She looked and looked and looked.

Here is a string for you. I want you to look and find all of your "lost coins." They look like this. *[Show child a Cheerio or Fruit Loop. Place 10 Cheerios or Fruit Loops in plain sight in different places in the room and have child search for them. As the child* *finds each one, add it onto their string.]*

In Jesus' story, when the woman found her lost coin, she was so excited that she called all her friends and had a big party. Now we can have a party too! *[Sit down with your child and enjoy eating the pieces of cereal off the string.]*

Theme: God's Word

Bedtime Rituals

At bedtime, say good night to your child's favorite toys as you make the circuit around his/her bedroom. *Tell each toy that Jesus will send His angels to watch over each of them while they sleep. Say something like this:]* "Good night, Pooh Bear; it's time to go to sleep. Jesus will send His angels to watch over us while we sleep tonight. Good night, Thumper Bunny. Jesus is going to send His angels to watch over you while you sleep too. Good night, Big Dog. *[Lay your little one in bed after hugs and kisses and remind him/her that Jesus* will watch over him/her too.]

Theme: Healthy Body

#32

Touch

T ouch is vital to children's well-being. It can help calm your little ones at bedtime. This is a particularly good worship activity for bedtime, or right after a bath. As you dry each little body part, or as you rub it before bedtime, say, "This is Michael's head. Thank You, God, for making Michael's head just perfect with two little ears, exactly in the right place, and soft fuzzy hair, and a little nose right in the front where it belongs!" Rub his little back and thank God for his strong back. Thank God for his chest and his tummy as you rub them. Rub his arms and each little finger and toe. Rub each body part, name it, and thank God for it. This will help your child develop a strong healthy body image, as well as realizing that each body part was made by God especially for him. Later, as your little one gets used to the routine and knows what's coming next, you can say, "Thank You, God, for _____" and have your child name each body part as you rub it. Remember to use only a light touch. Toddlers rarely appreciate a deep massage.]

Theme: Healthy Body

"No!"

When babies say "No," they're simply exercising the increased control they gain over their world when they shake their head and use this new and exciting word. Capitalize on this during your worship. Ask your child lots of questions to which "No" is the appropriate answer.]

Jesus likes it when I say "No!" when I think about taking my little brother's toys away from him. [Allow the child to answer, "No!"] Or how about when Mommy calls me and I think I would rather stay and play with my toys? [The toddler answers again, "No!" This can work like an antiphonal reading of the psalms.]

Other questions could include:

"When I'm tempted to stay up late past my bedtime . . ."

"When I'm tempted to eat too much candy and I know it will be bad for my tummy . . ."

"When I'm tempted to bite my brother, hit my friend, throw my toys at someone."

[Reinforce in the child's thinking that he/she has control of his/her behavior and can choose to say "No!" and act in a way that would make Jesus proud of him/her.]

Theme: Self-control

#34

Affirmation Ministry

Materials: *blank 3" x 5" index cards, stickers*

If children are old enough to recognize and enjoy people outside the family, they're old enough to learn the ministry of affirmation. Any time of year is appropriate for affirmation, although special days such as Valentine's Day or Thanksgiving give a special opportunity to express appreciation to those around you. Provide the child with index cards and stickers and help him/her decorate them. Draw a line down the middle of the back of the card, dividing it into two halves. On one half write the address of the person the child has chosen, and on the other half put a message from the child, such as "I really like you," "On this Thanksgiving Day I'm thanking God for you," "I just want you to know you're a special friend," etc.]

Theme: Affirming Others

Bugs, Part 1

Materials: *a few realistic plastic or rubber bugs*

Place all the bugs in a paper bag, and let your child reach in and pull them out, one at a time. Have the child try to name the bug or, if your toddler is very young, name the bug for him/her. And then remind your toddler, "Jesus made grasshoppers; Jesus made bumblebees," etc.]

Theme: Nature

#36

Bugs, Part 2

Materials: *an assortment of plastic bugs*

Jesus loves the bugs. He knew that some bigger animals and lots of birds would try to eat the bugs. So He gave them a special way to hide. It's called camouflage. He made some bugs green so they could hide on leaves and not be seen. He made some bugs brown so they could hide against wood. He made some bugs black.

[As you explain each color, place the bug against something of that color in your room and show how the bug blends in and is not as easy to see. Then allow your preschooler to find a place for each bug to hide in the room where it will be camouflaged. Place all your bugs in plain sight so they will be easy to retrieve afterward. For an advanced preschooler, hide all the bugs in camouflaged spots in plain sight before worship and let the child go on a bug hunt, collecting all the bugs. Remind him/her that Jesus gave the bugs camouflage because He loves the bugs too and wants to protect them.]

Theme: Nature

Sabbath Candles

Materials: *candles*

Preschoolers are fascinated by fire. Candles are a good way to capitalize on this and teach fire safety at the same time. Use short, stocky candles, or votive candles in small glasses, so that the candles can't tip over and cause a fire. On Friday evenings, especially during the winter season when sundown came early, we would turn off all the lights in the house. As the house started to get dark, we would light all our special Sabbath candles and set them around the living room. We would welcome the Sabbath by singing our special Sabbath songs. This enforces in the toddler's mind how special the Sabbath is. Preschoolers love to blow candles out, so before your child goes to bed, allow him/her to blow out all the Sabbath candles. Promise your child he/she can light them again next week when the Sabbath begins.]

Theme: Sabbath Is Special

#38

The Holy Spirit and the Wind

Materials: *a cardboard juice can with both metal ends removed, crepe paper streamers (or you can use light fabric or pieces of yarn or string)*

Have your preschooler help you wash and dry the juice can. Then using masking tape, tape or staple the streamers to one end of the can. Firmly tape or staple a loop at the other end for hanging. If you have a preschooler who enjoys coloring, have him/her color paper decorations and then tape or staple them firmly in place. Hang the can outside a window and watch it with your preschooler.]

Which way do the streamers point? That is the direction the wind is blowing.

We can't see the wind, but we can tell that it's there because of what it does to our wind sock. The Holy Spirit is like the wind. We can't see Him. We can see only what He does. But we know He is there, because God promised that the Holy Spirit is with us all the time, just like the air around us. Even though we can't see Him, when we see what He does we know He is with us, and we can tell God "Thank You!"

Dear God, thank You for the Holy Spirit, who is with us always.

#39

Theme: God's Word

Looking Forward to Sabbath

Create a calendar for your toddler that can be affixed to the refrigerator. A preschooler's calendar should have only the seven days of the week on it—30 days is a little overwhelming. Buy a special magnet for marking the day of the week. Decorate the calendar with pictures of what is done on each day—a little church on Sabbath, perhaps a picture of the whole family together on Sunday, if it's a day when Mom and Dad don't have to work. Put in any other familiar appointments or rituals that will help your child identify the days. Each morning help your child move the magnet to the correct day. Say, "Today is Tuesday. That means we have only a few more days till Sabbath. Let's count them: one, two, three, four. Four more days till Sabbath!" If your child already knows how to count, then name the days until Sabbath. "Today is Tuesday, so we have only Wednesday, Thursday, and Friday until it's Sabbath again!" This not only helps your toddler look forward to Sabbath as a special day, but helps him/her learn to count to seven and learn the days of the week.]

Theme: Sabbath

#40

Thank-you Clothesline

Materials: *rope, yarn, twine, or string, and clothespins*

A Christian writer once said, "To pray without ceasing is to develop a permanent attitude of gratitude." A "thank-you clothesline" will help your child develop an attitude of gratitude. This may be done with light string, yarn, or twine attached to a wall or bulletin board, or it can be done with a piece of rope strung between two chairs. Ask the child what kinds of things he/she wants to thank God for today. Using a heavier clothesline allows you to clip up things like warm socks, a favorite small stuffed animal, or other things for which your child is thankful. If you use a light string, you may want to clip up pictures only. If your preschooler is old enough, allow him/her to go through old magazines or seed catalogs and cut out pictures of things for which he/she is thankful. Then clip them up on the clothesline. At worship time, help your child say a prayer, thanking God for each item on his/her "thankful clothesline." Preschoolers enjoy this and will want to repeat this activity again and again, using different items each day.]

#41

Theme: Prayer

Adam and Eve's Job

Materials: *topiary form, small potted plant, pipe cleaner*

In the beginning God created Adam and Eve. He created a special garden home for them to take care of and make pretty. We're going to do one of Adam's jobs and make our garden pretty.

[Select a topiary shape. Garden shops and craft stores sell wired topiary forms, or you can create your own from florist wire or bendable wire clothes hangers. You can make spheres, circles, hearts, cones, or spirals. Select a small potted plant to train. Ivy is a good choice, or any vine whose tendrils are long and easily trained. Place the form into the soil in the pot and plant the ivy plant around it. Weave the ivy pieces into the form. You may use pipe cleaners to help secure the tendrils loosely to the form. Help your child water the plant every day and continue wrapping the plant into the form until it covers the wire. You can also make herb garden topiaries. Sweet myrtle, rosemary, and lavender are especially good for this. Have your child color paper, or use aluminum foil, to decorate the pot. Place a flower in your plant or at the top of your topiary when it has grown into the desired shape.]

Theme: God's Word/Nature

#42

Fruit Basket Centerpiece

Materials: *brightly colored ribbon, several pieces of fruit*

Help your child tie bows around several different pieces of fruit. Some fruits may be hard to tie ribbon around, so use a piece of scotch tape to secure the ribbon to the bottom of the fruit where no one will notice. Have toddler put his/her finger in the middle as you tie the bow on top. Then give him/her a bowl and allow him/her to arrange the fruits as a table centerpiece of some of God's special gifts. As you put each piece of fruit in the bowl, say, "Thank You, God, for bananas! Thank You, God, for oranges! Thank You, God, for apples! Thank You, God, for lemons!" These centerpieces can last several days, and your child can open the presents by removing the ribbon and eating the fruit. In this way, the child can have one of God's presents every morning for breakfast.]

Theme: God's Gifts

Snowman

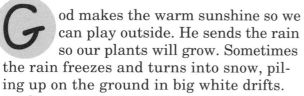

Materials: *a sock, some yarn or string, water-soluble markers*

God makes the warm sunshine so we can play outside. He sends the rain so our plants will grow. Sometimes the rain freezes and turns into snow, piling up on the ground in big white drifts.

Some people don't like snow. But everything God sends is good. When it snows we can make snowmen by rolling the snow into big balls and stacking them on top of each other. Today we're going to make a pretend snowman.

[Stuff the sock loosely with any type of stuffing material or dried beans. Secure the ends carefully so the stuffing won't spill out. Help the child tie string or yarn around the sock in two places to give the appearance of three stacked balls. Make the top one the snowman's head, a little smaller than the others. Fold the leftover cuff of the sock down around the top ball to make it look like the snowman's hat. Add button eyes—or draw them on with markers. Thank God for whatever weather you are having that day, because no matter what kind of weather God sends, we know He loves us and we can have fun in it.]

Theme: Nature

Devotion

#44

Jesus Loves Me

Materials: *florist wire, cranberries or popcorn*

Have your child poke a length of florist wire through the cranberries (or popcorn) until the wire is almost full. Then bend the wire into a heart shape and clip off the bare ends of wire. Your child can hang the heart in his/her room as a reminder that Jesus loves him/her. Sing "Jesus Loves Me." Cranberry and popcorn hearts can also be hung outside to help feed the birds during wintertime.]

Theme: Jesus' Love

David's Harp

Materials: *small box, scissors, four rubber bands long enough to stretch around the box, paint*

H*ave child paint box. Cut a wide hole in the top. Stretch rubber bands around box. Make sure each rubber band crosses the hole. Slide a pencil under the rubber bands on either side of the hole. Place one pencil parallel with the edge of the box. Angle the other pencil so that the length of each rubber band stretched between the two pencils is different. Allow child to pluck the four rubber bands. Notice that each one makes a different note.]*

We don't know exactly what David's harp was like, but we know he used it to play songs while he watched his sheep. He made up lots of songs and sang them to let God know how much he loved Him.

Let's see if we can make up a song, using the notes we can play on our harp, to show God how much we love Him.

[Help child make up a simple praise song, such as "I love Jesus, and He loves me," using the notes on the harp.]

Theme: God's Word

God's Gifts

Materials: *stick-on bow*

R emove the backing from the stick-on bow so it's ready to stick, and ask the child what he/she would like to thank God for. Child may place the bow on anything that he/she considers something God gave for which he/she is thankful. The bow may be placed on furniture, thanking God for comfortable places to sit; on favorite toys or books; on the high chair, food items, or even on Mommy or Daddy. Have a short prayer, thanking God for providing the item the child has chosen, as well as everything else we need in order to

live happy healthy lives.]

#47

Theme: Thankfulness

Fishers of Men

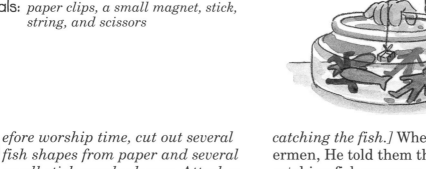

Materials: *paper clips, a small magnet, stick, string, and scissors*

Before worship time, cut out several fish shapes from paper and several small stick people shapes. Attach a paper clip to each fish and each stick person. Place the fish in one bowl, and the stick people in another. To make a fishing pole, tie one end of the string to the stick, the other end to the magnet.]

When Jesus first met Peter, Andrew, and John, they were fishermen. They caught fish for a living. Let's see how many fish we can catch. [Let the child go "fishing" by lowering the magnet into the bowl and catching the fish.] When Jesus met the fishermen, He told them they wouldn't be catching fish anymore. He was going to make them fishers of men. This didn't mean they would go out in their boats and catch men, instead of fish, in their nets. It meant they would preach the good news about Jesus to other people and bring them to meet Him.

[Teach the child to sing, "I Will Make You Fishers of Men," and use the magnet to go fishing for men in the other bowl.]

Theme: God's Word

#48

A Hole in the Roof

Materials: *two pencils, paper, tape or glue, a medium-size cardboard box or a Lincoln Log building set, a small toy person*

Once there was a man who was so sick he couldn't get up or walk or jump. Jesus was teaching near where the man lived. Since he couldn't go see Jesus by himself, his friends made a bed they could carry and took him on it.

[Use two pencils, paper, and glue or tape to make a "litter," and place one of the child's toy people on the stretcher.]

But when they got to the house *[use a large cardboard box turned upside down for the house, or build a house out of Lincoln Logs, making sure to use slats for the roof],* the crowds were so big they weren't able to get inside with their friend's bed.

What could they do? They decided to make a hole in the ceiling *[cut a hole in the top of your cardboard box, or remove the slats from your Lincoln Log house]* and lower the man and his bed through the roof.

The people were pretty surprised to see a man coming down through the ceiling. But Jesus wasn't surprised. He healed him and made him all better.

I'm sure the man remembered to thank his friends afterward for taking him to Jesus.

#49

Theme: God's Word

A Fight in the Night

One night Jacob was praying. He was very worried because he had had a fight with his brother and wondered if his brother would try to attack him.

Suddenly somebody jumped on him! *[Pounce on your child and wrestle gently.]* They rolled over and over, wrestling. Jacob was afraid. It was nighttime. He couldn't see the person he was wrestling with, but he thought it might be his brother.

They wrestled all night until it was almost morning. Then Jacob realized it wasn't his brother at all. In fact, it wasn't even anyone who wanted to hurt him. He was wrestling with God!

Jacob stopped fighting and just hung on to God, hugging Him tightly. He realized God wasn't going to hurt him. God was his friend. He loved God. It was a wonderful surprise, and Jacob knew, after wrestling with God all night, that God would be with him and that everything would be OK. He didn't have to worry anymore.

Theme: God's Word

#50

Brave Queen Esther

Materials: *colored paper, markers, sequins for jewels (optional), empty paper towel roll or stick, aluminum foil*

One day the king of Persia held a beauty contest. The winner would become the queen. Esther won! *[Make a crown out of paper and decorate with sequins for your little queen to wear.]* But she didn't tell anybody that she was Jewish and worshiped God. She kept that a secret.

One day a very bad man named Haman convinced the king to kill all the Jews in Persia. This meant all of Esther's family would be hurt. She decided she would go ask the king to save her people.

Esther was afraid, but she knew that God wanted her to be brave. She put on her best clothes and her crown, and went to see the king. As she stood in front of the king she said a secret prayer to God.

[Cover a paper towel roll or stick with aluminum foil to make a shiny scepter.]

God answered her prayer, and the king smiled. He held out his golden scepter. Esther told him of the plan to hurt her people. The king loved Esther and made a new law that not one of the Jews could be hurt. God was very happy with Esther for being so brave.

#51

Theme: God's Word

Jesus and the Children

J esus was a wonderful storyteller. The children liked to be close to Jesus when He told stories. They wiggled through the crowd and came up next to Him. But some of the grown-ups thought Jesus was too important to have children around.

"Take these children away!" they said. "Jesus is too important to be bothered with children. This is a grown-up meeting."

When Jesus heard this, He said, "No, let the children come. The kingdom of heaven belongs to people who are like these children."

He picked some of the children up so that they could sit on his lap. I wish I could sit on Jesus' lap, don't you?

[Sing "Jesus Loves the Little Ones Like Me, Me, Me." Put a bathrobe over a straight-backed chair so it looks like the front of a person. Place a picture of Jesus at the top so it looks like His head is coming out of the neck of the bathrobe. Allow your child to sit on the chair "on Jesus' lap," and place the arms of the bathrobe around him/her. You can cut out paper hands and pin them to the sleeves, if you like.]

Theme: Jesus Loves Children

#52

The Good Shepherd, Part 1

The Bible says that Jesus is our good shepherd. But shepherds sometimes have sheep who forget to follow, and who aren't always obedient. Sometimes one of the sheep wanders off and gets lost.

When a sheep doesn't have a shepherd to follow, it can get into all kinds of trouble. It can get its wool caught on pricker bushes. It can fall in the water or fall off a cliff. That sheep could even get stuck between two big rocks. But Jesus is such a good shepherd that He always goes and looks for His sheep. He looks and looks until He finds it.

[Play "lost sheep" and allow your child to hide in different places in the room. Then be the shepherd and call your little sheep, looking and looking until you find it. When you find your little lamb, pick it up and snuggle it close. Say, "I'm so glad that I found you; you are so important to me." Explain that we are just as important to Jesus, and that He loves us so much.]

#53

Theme: God's Word

The Good Shepherd, Part 2

I am gentle too!

Jesus is like a good shepherd. Shepherds have to be gentle with their sheep. If they hurt them, they will be afraid of them and run away.

Jesus was always gentle with people. He never hit people or hurt their feelings. Jesus was so gentle that even little children climbed up on His lap while He told them stories.

We need to learn to be just like Jesus. Since He was gentle with other people, we need to be gentle too. That means not shoving or hitting anybody or grabbing things away from them.

[Sing these words to the tune of "Happy, Happy Home."]

"Jesus was a gentle man. I am gentle too.
I am gentle too. I am gentle too.
Jesus was a gentle man.
I am gentle too. I am gentle too."

[Encourage your child to make up other words describing the type of man Jesus was when He was here on earth, such as: "Jesus was a happy man; I am happy too; Jesus was a prayerful man, I am prayerful too; or Jesus always trusted God, I can trust God too."]

Theme: God's Word
LHFJ-10

#54

The Good Shepherd, Part 3

I n the Bible Jesus is called the Good Shepherd. Shepherds take good care of their little lambs. They lead them where they need to go and keep them away from dangerous places where they could get hurt. A shepherd takes them where the water is calm so they can drink without getting knocked over or falling in the water.

Sheep follow close to their shepherd because they know if they stay with him/her they will be safe. This way they never have to be afraid.

[Play "follow the shepherd" and take turns being the shepherd. Have child follow closely behind the shepherd wherever he/she leads.]

#55

Theme: God's Word/Nature

Healing a Crippled Man

Materials: *money pouch, ace bandage*

O ne day Peter and John were on their way to the temple-church to pray. Many people who were crippled or hurt sat next to the Temple gates and asked people for money as they went by. They were not able to work to earn money to buy food.

As Peter and John went into the Temple, a crippled man asked them, "Can you give me some money?"

Peter and John said, "We don't have any money, but we can give you what we do have."

John reached down and grabbed the man by the hand and said, "By the power of Jesus Christ, stand up and walk." And he pulled the man up to his feet.

The man was so excited. He jumped up and down and shouted for joy. Let's pretend you are the crippled man.

[Give the child a little pouch to hold out as he/she asks for money. An ace bandage wrapped on one leg makes a very convincing crippled person. When you help your child to his/her feet in the name of Jesus, help him/her jump up and down and sing praises to Jesus.]

Theme: God's Word

#56

The Runaway

Materials: *money pouch*

J esus told His friends this story about a big brother who was happy at home, but the little brother decided to run away. He asked Daddy for some money, and he left. Daddy was very sad.

Soon the boy had spent all his money. He was cold and hungry. He found a job feeding pigs that gave him a little bit of money. But he was still so hungry that he ate the pigs' food.

These pigs are better off than I am, he thought. *They have food and a warm barn to stay in at night. I want to go home.*

When Daddy saw his son coming, he ran down the road to meet him. He hugged him and kissed him and had a big party to welcome his son back home.

[Give child a small bag of pennies as he/she leaves. As soon as he/she turns around to come back toward you, run and grab him/her, pick him/her up, giving kisses, saying, "Welcome home!"]

God is so sad if we decide to run away. But as soon as we start to come back, He gets so happy that the Bible says there is a big party in heaven. God loves us so much!

#57

Theme: God's Word

Jesus Makes a Mommy Happy

One day Jesus and His friends met some people coming out of a village called Nain. They were all crying. They were carrying a box with a boy in it who had died. The boy's mommy was especially sad because her husband had died before, and now her only son had died. She was all alone.

Jesus felt very sad for the mommy. He stopped and told her gently, "Don't cry." Then He went over and touched the dead boy. "Young man, wake up," He said. Even though the boy was dead, he heard Jesus' voice, because it was the voice of God.

The dead boy sat up. He wasn't dead anymore! His body was all well and healthy. His mommy hugged him and kissed him. She was so happy to see he was alive again. She thanked Jesus for giving her back her boy and making her life happy again.

Jesus was so kind. He cared about her feelings. He cares about our feelings too, and He wants us to be happy.

[Take turns role-playing, being the dead boy and coming to life when Jesus says to wake up.]

Theme: God's Word

#58

The Perfect Frog

Materials: *a plastic frog, a picture of a frog, or a real frog for the child to look at*

Frogs don't always look like this. A frog starts out as a little egg with no shell. When God looks at the egg, He doesn't say, "What a silly-looking frog." He says, "This is a perfect frog egg."

When the egg hatches, the little frog is called a tadpole, but it doesn't have any legs. *[Have child pretend to be an egg. Then have him/her hatch, keeping hands at sides and legs together.]* A tadpole has to wiggle its body to swim. *[Have child wiggle.]* But God looks at it and says, "What a perfect little tadpole!"

The tadpole keeps growing, and soon both its back legs and front legs start to grow. *[Allow child to start kicking legs.]* Now it looks like a real frog and uses all its legs to swim. *[Help child pretend to swim.]*

Now the frog can also come out of the water and hop around on land. *[Have the child hop.]* And God looks at it and says, "At last! You've become a perfect frog!"

Even though you started out as a tiny baby who couldn't walk and had to wear diapers and couldn't even feed yourself, God is happy with you, because He sees that you are just right for that time in your life.

#59

Theme: Nature

Plagues of Egypt

Materials: *small plastic animals, a large bowl of ice cubes*

his activity is best done outside. Place the plastic animals on the ground.]

For a while God's people were slaves in Egypt. They had to work very hard, and they were treated very badly. God sent Moses to rescue them. Moses told Pharaoh, "God says to let His people go."

But Pharaoh said, "No!"

So God told Moses, "I am going to send some terrible plagues on Egypt. One of them will be a plague of hailstones."

Hailstones are chunks of ice that fall from the sky. Usually hailstones are very small. But the hailstones God sent on Egypt were big! *[Drop ice cubes on plastic animals a few at a time. Allow your child to drop several on the animals. Hit all of the people and animals that aren't inside for shelter.]* It was a terrible plague! It hurt many Egyptians, and it killed many of their animals.

God loved His people and did not want them to be treated unkindly. This is why He sent plagues on Egypt.

Theme: God's Word

#60

Blood on the Door

Materials: *a small bowl of red paint, a paintbrush, and a large cardboard box*

[*This activity is best done outside.]* Pretend we are a slave family in Egypt. We work very hard for Pharaoh, but still he is mean to us. Moses told us we will leave Egypt tonight. It is so exciting, but Pharaoh still says we can't go. *[Cut a hole in the cardboard box for a door.]* Pretend this is our house, and this is the door.

God is sending the angel of death throughout Egypt to kill the oldest child in every home. But if we paint the blood of a lamb around our door the angel will pass over our house, and the oldest child will be safe.

Should we obey Moses? Yes! *[Help child paint red paint on both sides and across the top of the door.]* There. Now our house has blood all around the door, just as Moses said we should do. Now the angel of death will skip our house.

This is just what happened in Egypt, and all of God's people, who were obedient and painted their doorposts, were safe. And they did leave Egypt that night too!

Jesus was our Lamb; we don't have to paint blood on our doors anymore! His guardian angels will protect everyone in our house, because we love Him.

#61

Theme: God's Word

The Feast of Purim

Materials: *chalk*

ince the time of Queen Esther, the Israelites celebrate a holiday called Purim. Purim remembers how Queen Esther saved the Israelites from their enemies.

The king of Persia was looking for a new wife. He choose a beautiful Israelite girl named Esther. But no one, not even the king, knew she was one of God's people.

A very bad man named Haman tricked the king into making a law that said all the Israelites could be killed.

Esther bravely went to the king and asked him to save the lives of her people. The king agreed, and none of God's people were killed.

When the Jews celebrate Purim, they always tell the story of beautiful Queen Esther to their children. *[Use colored chalk to draw Queen Esther on the sidewalk—crown, scepter, the king, etc.]*

Theme: God's Word

LHFJ-11

#62

The Dedicated Daughter

Materials: *pearl barley, straw, basket, paper plate or construction paper*

N aomi and Elimelech had two sons, Mahlon and Chilion. When they were grown up, Mahlon married a woman named Ruth, and Chilion married a woman named Orpah. But a sad thing happened. Elimelech, Mahlon, and Chilion all got sick and died. Naomi, Ruth, and Orpah had no one to take care of them.

Naomi decided to move back to where she had lived when she was younger. She told Ruth and Orpah to go back to their families too. But Ruth knew Naomi was too old to work. She had no one to take care of

her or help her get food.

Ruth went to work in the barley fields. The man who owned the field told the men working in the fields to leave extra barley for Ruth. At the end of the day she took it home to Naomi. That way, she and Naomi had something to eat.

[Drop pieces of dried grain and straw around the room and let child pretend to be Ruth, picking up all the leftover straw. Give the child a basket to carry the straw in. Or use pearl barley on a plate to show the kind of food Ruth brought home to Naomi.]

#63

Theme: God's Word

Heavenly Crown

Materials: *several bright colors of construction paper, Scotch tape (do not use glue)*

C*ut a crown from construction paper. Lay it flat. Cut out several large "jewels" from contrasting colors of construction paper. Put a loop of tape on the back of each jewel so the edges can be pulled back to see the crown underneath. Draw smiley faces on the crown beneath each jewel to represent friends.]*

When we go to heaven Jesus will give us a jeweled crown to wear. And *your* crown will be different from everyone else's crown!

Do you know what the jewels are for? They are not because we had lots of money while we lived here on earth. And they are not because we were very good. Each jewel stands for somebody we told about Jesus. *[Pull each jewel up.]* Peekaboo! There's somebody you told about Jesus. *[Look under next jewel.]* Peekaboo! There's somebody else you told about Jesus. The people who have the most jewels in their crown in heaven will be the people who told the most people about Jesus.

Jesus wants our friends to know He loves them too. Let's tell somebody about Jesus today!

Theme: God's Word

#64

Mixed-up Bible Stories

T his activity is for older preschoolers who know their Bible stories.]
 There is something wrong with each sentence. Find the mistake and say what the correct ending should be.

 1. Baby Moses' mother wanted to hide him from Pharaoh, so *he was swallowed by a whale*.

 2. Baby Jesus didn't have a bed to sleep in the night He was born, *so his mother put him in a basket in the river*.

 3. Jonah didn't want to do what God said, so *his mother laid him in a manger*.

 4. Adam and Eve *escaped from Egypt*.

 5. Moses and the children of Israel *ate the fruit from the tree God had said not to eat from*.

 [Make up more mixed-up Bible stories for your child.]

Theme: God's Word

Mixed-up Tails

T his activity is appropriate for more advanced preschoolers who know their animals.]

There is something wrong with each sentence. Find the mistake and say what the correct ending should be.

1. The dog has a *tail made of long feathers that helps him keep his balance when he flies.*

2. The cat has a *strong tail made of two upright fins that help her steer when she swims.*

3. The bird has a *long, furry tail that* she wags when she is happy.

4. The fish has a *tail made of long hair that he can swing up to get the flies off his back when they bite him.*

[Make up more mixed-up tail sentences for you child.]

Theme: Nature

#66

Mixed-up Animal Sounds

Woof Woof

Neigh Neigh

T*his activity is appropriate for advanced preschoolers who know their animals.]*

Listen to each sentence and correct the mistakes:

1. The dog *can't talk, but it can say Meow, meow.*

2. The horse *can't talk, but it can* say *Woof, woof.*

3. The cow *can't talk, but it can say Neigh, neigh.*

4. The pig *can't talk, but it can say Moo moo.*

5. I *can't talk, I can only say Oink, oink.*

6. The cat *can talk because Jesus made* it special.

[Think of other mixed-up animal sounds for your child to identify.]

Theme: Nature

The Getting-Ready Time

Materials: *honey*

John the Baptist lived by himself in the desert. He did not have very much money, so he didn't have nice clothes like you have. He wore a camel skin to keep warm. It was kind of rough and hairy, and it probably made John itchy.

John didn't have a lot of fancy food, either. The Bible says he lived on locusts and honey. The locusts may not have tasted that good, because God made sure John had honey to eat with them. *[Let your child dip a finger in honey and taste it.]* I'm sure John thanked God for honey every day.

John lived in the wilderness where he could get ready for a special job God wanted John to do when he grew up. John became a famous preacher who baptized many people. He even baptized Jesus before Jesus started His preaching ministry.

Living in the wilderness was John's getting-ready time. Now is *your* getting-ready time. God has a special job for you, just as he had a special job for John. And if you trust God through the getting-ready time, He'll make sure you have everything you need to be happy.

Theme: God's Word

#68

Sally's Locust Adventure

Sally saw a grasshopper sitting on her sunflower plant. She remembered the story of John the Baptist and how he ate locusts and honey. *I'm going to be just like John the Baptist and eat a locust,* she thought. She picked up the grasshopper and put it in her mouth. It made a yucky crunchy noise as she chewed it.

"Sally, stop! What did you put in your mouth?" cried Mama.

"A locust," said Sally.

"No, no!" said Mama. "Don't eat bugs. You should never eat anything you find out-side unless Mama tells you it is good to eat."

"But John the Baptist did," said Sally.

Mama laughed. "Many people believe John the Baptist was eating pods from a locust *tree*, not the insect. The locust pods are a little bit bitter, and that's probably why he ate them with honey."

[Point out things that are good to eat in the fruit bowl, refrigerator, breadbox, etc. If you have fruit trees, berry bushes, or a garden, point out anything that is good to eat. Tell the child, "Never, never eat anything else outside that Mama hasn't shown you is good to eat."

Theme: God's Word/Healthy Body

Real and Pretend

Materials: *blocks, toy horns*

It is important to tell the difference between true stories and pretend stories. When we tell someone something, we must tell them whether it is real or pretend. The stories you hear from the Bible about Jesus and His friends are true stories. Stories that tell about animals that walk and talk, or stories that tell about fairies and magic, are pretend stories.

See if you can tell which are the beginnings of true stories and which are pretend stories:

1. Once upon a time there was a goose named Gertrude, who always wore a red hat.

2. The Bible tells a story about a man and a woman named Adam and Eve.

3. Peter the rabbit and his brother Arthur always argued over who got to play in the carrot patch.

4. One night I dreamed I was the king of the whole world.

5. Last week I went to the grocery store with my mom.

Remember, Jesus always wants us to tell the truth. If we are telling a pretend story, we let people know it is pretend.

Theme: Telling the Truth

LHFJ-12

#70

I Can Help Jesus Now!

Tucker is a little boy who loves Jesus. He wants to do things for Jesus when he grows up.

Tucker's mother is a musician. She often plays the piano for church. She also plays beautiful songs on her harp for church. When Mama makes music for church, Tucker stands next to her and turns the pages for her as she plays. Tucker is already doing a special job for Jesus by helping his mom.

How about you? Do you want to do special things for Jesus? You don't have to wait until you are grown up. Ask your mom or dad if you can do something to help. Helping your mom and dad counts as doing something for Jesus. *[Give child a simple task to do to help, such as putting plates on the table, picking up toys, turning pages, etc.]*

Dear Jesus, I love You and I want to help You. Please show me how to do things that will make You happy now, while I'm little, and when I grow up. Amen.

#71

Theme: Being Helpful

The Missing Dishes

Materials: *several dishes*

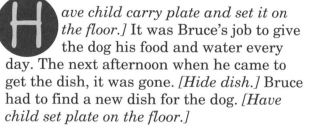ave child carry plate and set it on the floor.] It was Bruce's job to give the dog his food and water every day. The next afternoon when he came to get the dish, it was gone. *[Hide dish.]* Bruce had to find a new dish for the dog. *[Have child set plate on the floor.]*

The next day when he went to get the dog's dish, it was gone again. *[Hide dish.]* "Now I have to get you another bowl," said Bruce. *[Have child set plate on the floor.]*

The next day the dish was missing again! *[Hide plate.]* This time when Bruce set the food out for his dog, he watched from a window. *[Have child set plate on the floor.]*

Carefully the dog picked up the dish and ran down the steps and off toward the woods. Bruce followed him. There he found another dog whose leg was caught in a trap. Bruce's dog had been sharing food every day with the dog caught in the trap.

Bruce and his grandma helped take the dog out of the trap and bandaged the hurt leg.

God wants us to be kind to everyone and everything, especially when they are hurt.

Theme: Nature

#72

Following the Leader

Materials: *Picture of geese flying in "V" formation, a close-up picture of a goose, or take children to a pond or river where there are geese they can feed.*

During the summer geese can live just about anywhere. But when it starts to get cold, they fly to warm places where they can find enough food.

When geese fly away, we call it migrating. Each goose doesn't migrate by itself. It would be easy to get lost. And it could be attacked.

But geese don't fly in a big, confused flock, either, bumping into each other and getting in each other's way. They fly in a very orderly group that looks like a giant "V" behind a leader. No one teaches geese to fly this way. They do it naturally. God put something inside of them to tell them how to follow their leader when they migrate. God is good to geese. He's good to us, too.

Although each "V" group has a leader, it isn't the same leader all the time. Geese take turns. A leader who gets tired slows down, and another goose flies to the front of the "V." The rest of the geese honk encouragement to the new leader.

[Choose a leader and pretend to be geese. Flap your wings and follow each other. Remember to honk encouragement, and if there are more than two, fly in a "V" formation.]

#73

Theme: Nature

Zacchaeus

Materials: *large tin cans, twine*

Zacchaeus wanted to see Jesus, but he was too short to see over all the other people who wanted to see Jesus too. He tried jumping, but he still couldn't see. He climbed on a box, but he still couldn't see! Then Zacchaeus had a good idea. He climbed a tree and crawled way out on a branch that hung out over the road.

When Jesus got right underneath the tree, He stopped and looked up. Jesus said, "Zacchaeus, come down; I want to eat lunch at your house today."

Zacchaeus was so happy! Not many peo-ple liked him, but Jesus did. Zacchaeus was short, but that didn't matter to Jesus.

Sometimes it's hard being short. Jesus likes short people. And the best thing about being a short kid is that Jesus is still busy making you grow taller.

[Activity: Help child sit up on a tree branch to act out the story of Zacchaeus. Or use two large empty tin cans. Poke four holes in the top and thread twine in loops through the holes so your child can hold on to the twine as handles and use the cans as walking stilts to pretend to be taller.

Theme: God's Word

#74

Hunting With a Camera

Materials: *a small disposable camera*

Today we are going hunting. But we're not going hunting with a gun—we're going to shoot animals with a camera. That way, the animals won't get hurt, and we will have pictures to put in our "thankful book." *[See devotion number 16.]* Let's see how many live things we can find that Jesus made.

[Teach the child how to take pictures with the disposable camera. Encourage him/her to take pictures of birds, trees, small animals, and even ants, grasshoppers, and other insects. Use up the whole roll.

Children have a very short attention span, so it's most effective if the pictures can be developed the same day, although you can send them away and look forward to getting them back in the mail. Allow child to put favorite pictures up on the refrigerator with magnets or mount them in little frames to hang on the wall. Child may also ask you to write messages on the back of pictures and send them to special people. This exercise will help child be more aware of all the living things around him/her.]

#75

Theme: Nature

Funny Faces

Materials: *paper plates, buttons, markers, yarn, sequins*

Today we are going to make funny faces.

[On the paper plates, let child make as many faces as he/she likes, then compare them. Although some may be better than others, point out that no matter how good our paper plate faces look, Jesus is much better at making real faces.]

Aren't you glad it was Jesus who made your face? Jesus makes our faces much better than anything we can do.

Theme: Healthy Body

#76

First-Aid Food

Materials: *paper cups (four ounces or smaller) or ice cube tray, plastic spoons or forks, fruit juice*

P*our different colors of fruit juice into paper cups. Place a plastic spoon in each one and put them in the freezer. They should freeze in about an hour.]*

God made lots of things that can help us when we get hurt. Today we're going to use something God made and learn how to help sore throats or small bumps or cuts in our mouth or on our lips. *[Take the frozen juice pops out of the freezer.]*

Yes, they look just like Popsicles, but they're good for sore throats. If you get hurt and bump your lip, they help the swelling go down too. But the best thing about God's first-aid helpers is that you don't have to be hurt to enjoy them. Let's have a frozen juice pop!

Theme: Nature

John the Baptist

Materials: *chalk*

Before John the Baptist started his job of telling people that Jesus was coming, he lived for a long time by himself in a country far away from cities and most people. He lived in the wilderness, near the river Jordan, where he preached and baptized people. He ate simple food, wore simple clothes, and talked to God a lot.

You're getting ready to do a job for God too. Right now you are growing up. Your job is to eat good food, wear simple clothes, and talk to God a lot, just as John the Baptist did. Except you don't have to live out in the wilderness all by yourself. You get to live with your family.

[Draw several chalk circles across your driveway. Make sure they are close enough so child can jump from circle to circle. Let child try to cross the Jordan River by jumping from rock (circle) to rock (circle). If he/she misses one of the circles say, "Whoops, you got wet!" Remind child that it's not a big deal. John the Baptist didn't mind getting wet in the Jordan. He stayed in the river all day when he was baptizing people. This activity will help child with large muscle group coordination.]

Theme: God's Word

LHFJ-13

#78

A Golden Crown for You

Materials: *lots of dandelions or daisies*

When Jesus comes and takes us to heaven, He is going to give us golden crowns to wear. But did you know we can wear crowns now? They aren't made of gold—they're made of flowers!

[Have your child pick lots of flowers with longer stems. You can put together a daisy or dandelion crown by making a small slit in the stem and slipping the stem of the next flower into it. Then make a slit in that stem and slip another flower through it until you have a chain long enough to make a crown. Children are delighted by daisy or dandelion
crowns. Remind them to pick only flowers in their own yard or flowers they have permission to pick, since neighbors don't always appreciate little ones picking their flowers.]

Theme: God's Word

Tongues, Part 1

Materials: *a cooperative cat or a piece of sandpaper*

If you touch your tongue *[have child touch his/her tongue],* you will find that it is soft and wet. But a kitty's tongue is different. If a kitty licks you, you will notice that a kitty's tongue is very rough, kind of like sandpaper. *[Let the child feel a piece of sandpaper with his/her finger.]*

Why do you think a kitty's tongue is different from yours? God knew kitties need to do different things with their tongues than you do with yours. You use your tongue for tasting food. Your tongue has lots of taste buds that tell you whether food tastes sweet, salty, or sour.

A kitty's tongue is used like a washcloth. The mama kitty licks her babies all over to clean them and comb their fur. Your mommy uses a washcloth and a comb and brush. *[Wash your child's face, then comb your toddler's hair with a comb and brush.]* Aren't you glad your mommy's tongue wasn't made for washing faces and combing hair? It would make you all sticky!

God made the kitty's tongue just right for taking care of little kitties. And He made your tongue just right for tasting food. Isn't God wonderful? He is so smart!

Theme: Nature

#80

Tongues, Part 2

Materials: *a picture of a dog, an adhesive bandage, antiseptic cream*

D ogs have big, sloppy, wet tongues, and when they lick you, you can feel kind of yucky sometimes. But dogs show us they love us by licking us.

You may notice that if you've been hurt, a dog will lick the sore spot. Some people think that's really gross and worry that germs will get in the wound from dog saliva. But God put something in dog saliva that actually kills germs and helps make hurts better.

Your saliva doesn't kill germs. God knew people would use other things when they got hurt, so when you get a little cut or sore place, Mommy washes it with water, and then puts antiseptic cream and a bandage on it. That's because you aren't a puppy. If you were a puppy, your mommy would just lick the sore place.

God knows exactly what each animal needs. He is so smart. He made dogs' tongues just the way they need to be for dogs, and He made your tongue just right for people.

#81

Theme: Nature

Seashells

Materials: *a small container of shells from the beach*

 ou can purchase shells in craft or nature stores if you do not live where you can pick them up yourself.]

God made two main types of seashells. He made one kind with a round opening that goes inside and curls round and round and round. Snails and other creatures live in these kinds of shells. They are called uni-valves. "Uni" means one. There is one hole in this type of shell.

The other kind of shell has two halves that fit together, protecting the sea creature on both sides. The shell has a hinge on onc side so the animal can open the shell when it eats, and close it again when it is scared or needs protection. These are called bi-valves. "Bi" means two. You can remember that this type of shell has two halves.

Aren't you glad that Jesus didn't make all shells exactly the same? If you look through these shells, you will see they are so different, and they have so many different colors. God used lots of imagination when He was creating our world. God is so awesome!

[Help your child pick and identify the univalves and separate the bivalve shells.]

Theme: Nature

#82

Adventures at the Beach

S ally loved running along the beach and getting sand between her toes. But what she liked best of all was picking up seashells. She had found several shells that she brought home in a bucket.

When she woke up the next morning, one of her shells was crawling across the table! What could make a shell crawl?

It was a univalve. *[See devotion number 82 for an explanation of univalve and bivalve shells.]* When she picked the shell up, she saw little legs sticking out the hole. A hermit crab was living in the shell.

Hermit crabs have a hard shell only on their legs. Their bodies are soft. God made them that way, but He taught them to be very smart. They find an empty univalve shell and put the soft part of their body inside. Then they can walk with their legs and carry the shell around with them. As they grow and get too big for their shell, they slip out of it and find a bigger shell to live in.

Look at your shells and sort out which ones could be a home for a hermit crab. Remember, hermit crabs can't live in bivalve shells, only in univalve shells.

Theme: Nature

#83

Sponges

Materials: *a sponge (preferably a real sea sponge, but if not available, use a human-made sponge from the grocery store)*

This is a sponge. Sponges are one of the neatest things God made. They live and grow in the bottom of the ocean. When they die, other sea animals use them as homes.

People who work as divers dive down in the ocean and collect sponges and bring them up from the ocean floor. They carefully clean them to get rid of all the slime and little sea creatures hiding inside, and then they sell them in stores.

Sponges are useful in cleaning our houses and are fun to play with in the bathtub.

[If you are using a human-made sponge, explain that God's idea of sponges was such a good one that people make artificial ones.] This is a rubber sponge. It doesn't cost as much as sponges that come from the ocean, but it is made with the same idea.

God is so smart, and He always has the best ideas. *[Let the child play with the sponge in a basin of water or in the bathtub.]*

Theme: Nature

Sea Animal Fun

Materials: *a double-sided suction pad used for holding soap on the side of a bathtub (can be purchased in most grocery or variety stores)*

The octopus doesn't have a body—just a head attached to eight legs. Its legs can stretch out long or pull back and get short, just like a rubber band.

Each leg has lots of little sucker pads. The octopus uses its sucker pads to hang on to rocks or shells that it catches for its dinner. This is how they work. *[Demonstrate with the soap holder pad. This works best if it's wet (an excellent bathtub activity). Wet the suction pad and stick it on to any smooth surface, then let child peel it off.]*

See how tightly it hangs on? An octopus can do that too. That's why it's important not to touch an octopus if you were to ever find one hiding at the beach. They can hang on to you, too. But you don't have to be afraid. Only a very tiny octopus can live near the beach.

Our God is so smart. He knew that the octopus with eight legs and no fingers would need a way to hang on to things. But I'm glad He gave me fingers. God knew what was the best for each one of His creatures, and He knows what's best for me.

Theme: Nature

#85

More Sea Animal Fun

Materials: *a jar of water, a bottle of India ink (food coloring will work if ink is not available)*

f using food coloring, mix several colors together in a small container to make a dark color.]

The octopus is very soft and feels wet, the way your tongue feels. Stick your tongue out and feel it with your finger.

The octopus doesn't have much protection from animals that might try to eat him. Eels especially like octopus for lunch. Eels look like snakes, but they are really a type of fish.

God gave the octopus a special way to protect itself from eels. The octopus has a little sac inside its head that contains a dark fluid that looks like ink. When he gets scared, he shoots the fluid into the water.

[Dump your ink or food coloring mixture into a jar of water.] It is just like this all around the octopus. The eel can't see where the octopus went. And the ink has something in it that makes the eel very sleepy. As the ink floats away in the water, the eel wakes up, but by then the octopus has found somewhere to hide.

God knows how to protect it from things that would hurt it. And God loves me and protects me, too. God is just awesome!

Theme: Nature

#86

Turtles

Materials: *laundry basket or box, a small turtle (real or plastic), a turtle picture*

Some turtles live in the ocean and grow very large. Others live on land and crawl around on dry ground. God gave turtles a round, hard shell for protection. If you tapped on a turtle shell with your fingernail it would make a clicking noise, but the turtle wouldn't feel anything. Its shell keeps it safe.

A turtle's head, feet, and tail stick out from its shell. But when something comes along that scares the turtle, it pulls everything all back inside its shell.

Let's play turtle. *[Use a laundry basket, a large basin, or cardboard box to put over the child's back. Have him/her crawl around, pretending to be a turtle. Jump up and say, "Boo!" and have child pull his/her head, arms, and legs back under shell.]*

Jesus loves the turtles He made, so He made sure they have a place to hide when they are scared. Jesus loves you too, and He will take care of you. But I'm glad we don't have to wear a hard shell. We wouldn't be able to move very fast, would we? Jesus knew how to make each creature just right.

#87

Theme: Nature

Crustaceans

Materials: *a shrimp or lobster (live or plastic) or a picture*

any grocery stores have a live lobster tank, or you may be able to purchase a large shrimp in the seafood section of your grocery store.]

This kind of animal is called a crustacean. It's easy to remember its name, because if you tap its shell with your fingernail it feels crusty. These animals are soft inside, but have a hard shell on the outside to protect them.

Some of the largest crustaceans in the ocean are called lobsters. There are smaller ones called shrimp. There is even a crustacean called crayfish that lives in streams and ponds.

The mother crustacean lays a whole cluster of eggs that stick together with slime. Then she uses her tail to hold the sticky ball of eggs close to her body so other hungry fish can't eat them. She will keep these eggs tucked under her tail until the little crustaceans are ready to hatch and swim away.

God cares about baby crustaceans. He cares about baby people, too. He gave you a mommy to take care of you and protect you until you are old enough to live by yourself. God thinks of everything.

Theme: Nature

#88

Blind Bartimaeus

Bartimaeus was blind. He couldn't go to work and earn money, because he couldn't see. So he sat on his mat outside the city of Jericho and asked people for money as they passed by. Then he would use the money to buy food.

[Put a blindfold on child and have him/her sit on a towel on the floor, like Bartimaeus. Give him/her a little dish to hold out for pennies.]

One day Bartimaeus heard that Jesus was coming to Jericho. He knew Jesus would be in a crowd, so he would have to shout loudly so Jesus could hear him. "Jesus, please help me!" he shouted at the top of his lungs. *[Have your child shout like Bartimaeus.]*

Jesus heard him and asked Bartimaeus what he wanted. "I want to see again," he said. "Please fix my eyes."

And Jesus did! *[Pull the blindfold off your child.]*

Bartimaeus was so happy and excited! He told everyone what Jesus had done for him. We should tell everybody about the good things Jesus does for us, too.

#89

Theme: God's Word

Guided by a Whale

Materials: *a laundry basket*

P[lace child in the laundry basket and have him/her pretend to be a scientist who's watching whales from a little boat.]

A group of scientists were studying whales. Every day they went out in their boat and watched the whales. They put microphones in the water so they could hear whale noises.

One day while the scientists were out in their boat, a very thick fog came up. They couldn't see where the land was or how to get back to it. Then they prayed and asked God to help them.

Suddenly, right next to their small boat, a whale came up. It blew a spout of water out of its airhole. Then it swam a little way away from the boat and spouted again. The scientists decided to follow the whale. It led the little boat back to the island they had come from.

Sometimes God uses other people to help us when we are in trouble. Sometimes He uses angels. And sometimes He uses even animals. But He always takes care of His people.

Thank You, God, for taking care of me. Amen.

Theme: Nature

#90

Presents

Materials: *paper plates, pictures or stickers, gift bows, coat hanger*

I like to get presents, don't you? God gave us lots of presents, but because they don't come all wrapped up with bows on them, sometimes we don't recognize what wonderful presents He's given us.

[Have child cut out pictures or use stickers or make drawings on paper plates of things for which he/she is thankful. Then turn the plates over and put gift bows on the front of them. Punch a hole in the top and hang several plates from a coat hanger, like a mobile. Look at each plate, one at a time. Ask, What's in this present? Turn the plate around and say, "Peekaboo! It's Mom [or flowers, etc.]!" Say a thank-You prayer for Mom.]*

#91

Theme: God Loves U

Just Ask

One day Aunt Esther had a problem with her doorbell. It rang and rang. She opened the door and looked outside, but nobody was there. *[Allow child to ring doorbell repeatedly.]* Then she looked closely and found a little seed wedged into the doorbell. The seed made the doorbell button stay pushed in so that it rang and rang. She pulled the seed out and the doorbell stopped. She refilled her bird feeders and went back in.

A few days later Aunt Esther's doorbell rang. She opened the door. No one was there.

She checked the doorbell. Again there was a little seed stuck there. The next time the bird feeders needed to be refilled, she watched from her window. A little bird flew over to the front door, carrying a seed in its beak. It pushed the sunflower seed into the space between the doorbell button and the wall. The doorbell rang and rang.

Aunt Esther laughed. God helped the bird learn how to ask when it needed something! God wants us to ask Him when we need something too. All we have to do is close our eyes and tell God what we need.

Theme: Nature

#92

Baby Cain

When Adam and Eve had to leave their beautiful garden home, they were very sad. God knew they were sad. He still loved them so much, even though they had disobeyed Him. So He sent them a special surprise to cheer them up. The surprise was the very first baby born in this world.

Adam and Eve loved Baby Cain. They played patty-cake with his little hands. *[Play patty-cake with child.]* They tickled his little feet. *[Tickle child's feet.]* They patted his little tummy. *[Pat child's tummy.]* And they

scratched his little head. *[Tousle child's hair.]*

Adam and Eve loved Baby Cain very much. They were hoping Baby Cain would be God's Son, who had promised to come and save them. Baby Cain wasn't God's Son, but every baby who was born on earth was special. Every mommy and daddy looked at their baby and thought, *Is this the one?*

Even though Baby Cain wasn't the Promised One, Adam and Eve loved him. They knew that he was a special gift from God, and that God still loved them.

#93

Theme: God's Word

The Armor of God

Materials: *plastic armor or picture of a Roman soldier in armor*

Jesus promised to protect us from Satan's mean traps. Jesus protects us just like armor if we ask Him. A Roman soldier wore a helmet to protect his head. He wore a breastplate to protect his chest. He wore a wide belt to protect his tummy, and shoes to protect his feet. He also had a big shield and a sword for fighting the enemy. Jesus has promised to protect us just like that.

[Sing to the tune of "London Bridge Is Falling Down."]

Jesus is my shield of faith, shield of faith, shield of faith.
Jesus is my shield of faith, I love Jesus.

[For other verses, substitute the following for "shield of faith":]

Jesus is my Spirit sword . . .
Jesus is my helmet too . . .
Jesus is my shoes of peace . . .
Jesus is my breastplate too . . .

Theme: God's Word

LHFJ-15

#94

God Is Very Good

T he Bible tells us that it makes God very happy when we praise Him and tell about how good He is. The Bible also tells us that we should think about God while we're playing, while we're walking, while we're eating, and even while we're resting in bed.

We can sing praises to God while we're doing all these things.

[Sing to the tune of "Row, Row, Row Your Boat."]

I sing while I play, God is very good.
Singing, playing, singing, playing,

God is very good.

[For other verses, substitute the following activities in the song: crawl, run, jump, swing, and bathe.]

#95

Theme: Praising God

I Love
the Lord

It's easy to love somebody when that person already loves us. The Bible tells us that God loved us first, even before we were born.

[Sing to the tune of "The Farmer in the Dell."]

I love the Lord
Because He first loved me.
I really love the Lord
Because He first loved me.

Theme: I Love Jesus

#96

I Love Jesus;
Yes, I Do!

 Jesus loves us so much, and He likes to hear us say that we love Him too.
[Sing to the tune of "Twinkle, Twinkle, Little Star."]
I love Jesus; yes, I do,
   and I know He loves me too.
Jesus loves my mom and dad,
   gave me everything I've had.
I love Jesus; yes, I do,
   and I know He loves me too.

#97

Theme: I Love Jesus

We Tell All the People

he Bible tells us that when we love Jesus, we'll get excited about Him and want to tell other people the good news.

[Sing to the tune of "The Wheels on the Bus Go Round and Round"]

We tell all the people God loves you,
God loves you, God loves you.
We tell all the people God loves you,
all through the town.

[For additional verses, substitute the following lines:]

We tell all the people Jesus saves . . .

We tell all the people He forgives . . .
We tell all the people love Him too . . .

Theme: Sharing Jesus' Love

#98

I Am Growing Just Like Jesus

When Jesus came to earth, He didn't come as a grown-up. No, He came as a tiny baby and had to grow up, just like you. He had to eat and play and take naps, just like you. Jesus learned to sing and pray to God. He learned to play nicely with His friends. And He was always kind. Jesus learned all about God from His mommy, just like you.

[Sing to the chorus of "The Battle Hymn of the Republic."]

I am growing just like Jesus.
I am growing just like Jesus.

I am growing just like Jesus.
Growing every day.
[For additional verses, substitute the following lines:]
I am singing just like Jesus . . .
I am praying just like Jesus . . .
I am playing just like Jesus . . .
I am learning just like Jesus . . .

#99

Theme: Learning to Be Like Jesus

Jesus Once Was 2, Like Me

Jesus came to this earth as a tiny baby, and He had to grow just like you. Jesus was 1 year old, just like you. Jesus was 2 years old, just like you. Jesus was 3 years old, just like you. *[Stop when you come to your child's age.]*

[Sing to the tune of "London Bridge Is Falling Down."]

Jesus once was 2 like me, 2 like me,
    2 like me.
Jesus once was 2 like me; I love Jesus.

[If you have other preschool siblings, you can sing additional verses: Jesus once was 5 like Don, etc.]

Theme: Jesus Was Like Me

#100

Praise, Praise, Praise the Lord!

When David was out watching his sheep, he sang lots of praise songs to God. He wrote some of them down, and we still have those songs in our Bible. They're called the Psalms. You can sing praise songs to God too. What do you want to thank Him for today? *[Fill in the blank in the song below.]*

[Sing to the tune of "Row, Row, Row Your Boat." Let each child pick something to thank God for.]

Praise, praise, praise the Lord!
Praise Him every day.

Thank Him for _____ .
Praise Him every day.

#101

Theme: Praise God

Joseph Was a Carpenter

Materials: *plastic carpenter's tools, sandpaper, a polishing rag*

When Jesus was a little boy, He was God's Son. But God gave Him a daddy here on earth to take care of Him too. The daddy's name was Joseph. Joseph was a carpenter. Jesus liked to help His daddy. He used tools like these, and sandpaper like this to make things smooth. He used polishing cloths to make things shiny. Pretend you are Jesus while we sing this song.

[Sing to the tune of "Old McDonald Had a Farm."]

Joseph was a carpenter; Jesus was his boy.

Jesus liked to help His dad. Worked all
    day with joy.
With a *pound, pound* here and a *pound,*
    pound there.
Here a *pound,* there a *pound,* every
    where a *pound, pound.*
Joseph was a carpenter; Jesus was his boy.
[For additional verses, substitute the following lines:]
With a *saw, saw* here . . .
With a *sand, sand* here . . .
With a *rub, rub* here . . .

Theme: Jesus Was a Helper

LHFJ-16

#102

Devotion

Samuel

Samuel's mommy prayed for him, even before he was born! She promised to give Him to God. Eli was the high priest at the tabernacle, and when Samuel was old enough, his mommy took him to live with Eli.

Samuel helped Eli with everything. He helped polish the lamps and the candlesticks and all the furniture in the tabernacle. He helped the priests knead the dough for the unleavened bread every week. He also helped the priests with the sheep.

Pretend you are Samuel as we sing this song. *[Sing to the tune of "Old McDonald Had a Farm."]*

> Eli was the Lord's high priest; Samuel was a boy.
> Samuel helped Priest Eli work, worked all day with joy.
> With a *rub, rub* here and a *rub, rub* there.
> Here a *rub,* there a *rub,* everywhere a *rub, rub.*
> Eli was the Lord's high priest; Samuel was a boy.

[For additional verses, substitute knead, knead / baa, baa, etc.]

#103

Theme: God's Word

Jesse

esse was David's daddy. He owned a lot of sheep. David was the youngest boy in the family, and it was his job to watch the sheep. David made sure the sheep got lots of green grass to eat, and he made sure they had plenty of water to drink. While he watched the sheep, he sang lots of praise songs to God.

[Sing to the tune of "Old McDonald Had a Farm."]

Jesse owned a lot of sheep; David was his boy.

David watched his daddy's sheep—

worked all day with joy.

With a *baa-baa* here and a *baa-baa* there,

Here a *baa*, there a *baa*, everywhere a *baa-baa*.

Jesse owned a lot of sheep; David was his boy.

[For additional verses, substitute the following:]

With some green grass here . . .

With some cool water here . . .

With a praise song here . . .

Theme: God's Word

#104

Adam

Adam was the world's first daddy. He had several children, but his very first son was Cain. Cain's job was to help in the garden, and he grew lots of fruit and vegetables.

[Sing to the tune of "Old McDonald Had a Farm."]

Adam was God's first-made man and
Cain was his boy.
Cain helped Daddy grow some food—
worked all day with joy.
With fresh fruit here and fresh
fruit there;

Here a fruit, there a fruit, everywhere a fresh fruit.
Adam was God's first-made man, and Cain was his boy.

[For additional verses, substitute the names of child's favorite fruits and vegetables.]

Theme: God's Word

Jonah

S *ing to the tune of "Jingle Bells."]*
"Go to preach, go to preach,
"Go to preach," God said *[shake finger emphatically].*

Jonah chose to run away—
Got on a ship instead *[make running motions with two fingers along your arm].*

Great big storm, great big storm,
Great big storm God sent *[make raining motions with fingers].*

Jonah tried to hide, but people threw him out instead *[make a throwing motion with both arms].*

Great big fish, great big fish,
Great big fish God sent *[make swimming fish motion with hand].*

Swallowed Jonah *[bring two hands together like big jaws],* swam back home *[make swimming motions with hand],*
And coughed him up again *[open hands again, like large jaws].*

"Go to preach, go to preach,
"Go to preach," God said *[shake finger emphatically].*

"Yes, I will!" cried Jonah *[nod head vigorously],* and he did just what God said.

Theme: God's Word

#106

God
Loves You

The Bible tells us that God loves us so much! God loves you, and He loves Mom and Dad. *[Mention each family member individually.]*
[Sing to the tune of "This Old Man."]
God loves you, God loves me, God loves our whole family.
God wants us to love each other too.
And we ought to love Him too.

#107

Theme: God's Love

Jericho Is Falling Down

od's people had come to a big city. It was named Jericho. Jericho had very high walls, and the people were afraid and didn't know how they could get inside the walls or fight the people who lived there.

God had them march around the city every day for six days. On the seventh day they marched around the city seven times, and then they shouted as loud as they could and blew their trumpets. God made the walls of Jericho fall down. God's people didn't have to fight anyone. They only had to do what God said. God is so good!

[Sing to the tune of "London Bridge Is Falling Down."]

Jericho is falling down,
Falling down,
Falling down.
Jericho is falling down;
God is winning!

[After singing "God is winning," cheer and clap.]

Theme: God's Word

#108

John the Baptist

 esus and John were cousins and were almost the same age. But before Jesus started telling the people about God, God told John to tell the people that Jesus, the Messiah, was coming soon and to get ready. John told people to get ready for the Messiah by asking God to forgive their sins, and he baptized them in the Jordan River. That's how he became known as John the Baptist.

[Sing to the tune of "Yankee Doodle."]
John the Baptist's getting ready,
Called folks to the river,

"Ask God to forgive your sins,
And follow your new Saviour."

Theme: God's Word

Jesus Visits the Temple

When Jesus was a little boy, He went with His mommy and daddy to the Temple. It took several days to get there, so lots of people traveled together. The roads were very crowded.

Jesus loved the Temple when He saw it. He asked the priests lots of questions and listened to what they were teaching till long after it was time to go home. Mary and Joseph missed Jesus, but thought He was traveling with one of his aunts or uncles or cousins or friends.

When Jesus was lost, He wasn't afraid. He was in the Temple listening to the priests and the teachers, but His mommy and daddy didn't know that and were very scared. They looked everywhere for Him and were so glad when they finally found Him.

[Sing to the tune of "Yankee Doodle."]
Jesus sat inside the Temple; He was
    busy listening.
Mom and Dad looked everywhere; their
    little Boy was missing.
Just as God helped Jesus' folks find Him
    when He was lost,
God will help your folks find you if you
    ever get lost.

Theme: God's Word
LHFJ-17

#110

Jesus Goes to the Synagogue

When Jesus was a little boy He went to the synagogue every Sabbath morning. ("Synagogue" is what Jewish people call their churches. There they sing songs and learn about God.) Jesus made it a habit to go worship God every Sabbath, and He wants us to make it a habit too.

[Sing to the tune of "Yankee Doodle."]
Jesus went to synagogue every
    Sabbath morning,
Sang some psalms and learned of God,
'Cause habits are important.

I go to my Sabbath school every
    Sabbath morning,
Sing some songs and learn of God,
'Cause habits are important.

#111

Theme: Jesus Went to Church

Follow Moses

G od's people were escaping from Egypt with Moses. Pharaoh was chasing them with his army. They came to a place where there was water in front of them. There were mountains on both sides. The Egyptians were behind them. What could they do? God made the water stop and roll back on both sides so they could walk across to the other shore. Then God let the water flow back together where it belonged as soon as the last of His people was safe. The water washed all the Egyptians away.

[Play follow the leader, and sing this song to the tune "Frère Jacques."]
Follow Moses, follow Moses
'Cross the sea, 'cross the sea.
We all have to hurry, we all have to hurry,
You and me, you and me.

Pharaoh's coming, Pharaoh's coming
'Cross the sea, 'cross the sea.
God put back the water, God put back
the water.
Now we're free! Now we're free.
[Clap your hands and cheer.]

Theme: God's Word

#112

No Bad Touching

Just Say **NO!**

When Joseph was a slave in Potiphar's house, he had to work very hard. One day a bad thing happened. Mrs. Potiphar wanted Joseph to be her boyfriend. She tried to touch Joseph. And she wanted Joseph to touch her. This made Joseph uncomfortable. He knew this was bad touching. He also knew that God wanted him to respect his body and not allow any bad touching or do any bad touching back. Joseph said, "No!" and ran away from Mrs. Potiphar. Even though Mrs. Potiphar was angry, Joseph did the right thing, and God was proud of him.

[Sing to the tune of "Frère Jacques."]
No bad touching, no bad touching.
Just say no; just say no!
I respect my body; I respect my body.
God said so; God said so.

#113

Theme: God's Word/Healthy Body

No Bad Smoking

God wants us to respect our bodies and take care of them. He wants us to do everything we can to keep them healthy. One thing that some people do that hurts their body is smoking.

When people smoke, they suck tobacco smoke into their lungs. This brings bad poisons inside their body that stay there a long time. Eventually it can make them sick.

There are no laws against smoking; each person gets to choose. But Jesus wants you to choose what will make your body the healthiest. It would make Jesus happy for you to choose never to smoke.

[Sing to the tune of "Frère Jacques."]
No bad smoking, no bad smoking.
Just say no; just say no!
I respect my body; I respect my body.
God said so; God said so.

Theme: Healthy Body

#114

Too Much Candy

God wants us to be careful about what we eat. Many people have a sweet tooth. That means they enjoy eating candy, cookies, cake, pie, ice cream, and other sweet things. God wants us to have yummy things to eat that make us happy, but we need to be careful not to eat too much of any one thing, because it can hurt us and give us a stomachache.

Most people don't have trouble with eating too many green beans, but a lot of people have problems knowing how much candy is too much.

[Sing to the tune of "Frère Jacques."]
Too much candy, too much candy.
Just say no; just say no!
I respect my body; I respect my body.
God said so; God said so.

Theme: Healthy Body

Floods Are Coming

God told Noah He was going to destroy the earth with a flood. He told Noah to build a big ship so that everyone who wanted to could escape.

God made animals come into the ark so they would be safe. But God didn't make the people come inside. The people had a choice.

Noah told them about God's plan for them to escape the flood. They could come inside, or they could choose to stay outside. But the flood would come anyway.

Only eight people chose to obey God. It was very sad.

[Sing to the tune of "Frère Jacques."]
Floods are coming, floods are coming.
Come inside; come inside.
God knows how to save us; God knows
     how to save us.
Come and hide; come and hide.

Theme: God's Word

#116

Storms Are Coming

Some people are afraid of storms. Jesus' disciples were afraid during a bad storm on the Sea of Galilee. Thunder can be very loud, lightning flashes are very bright, and the wind can blow very hard. But Jesus doesn't want us to be afraid. Jesus stood up in the disciples' boat and told the wind to stop blowing. Then He told the waves to be calm. And they obeyed Him!

Jesus knows it can be bright and loud, but He can take care of us through any storm, just as He took care of His disciples. We don't have to be afraid.

#117

[Sing to the tune of "Frère Jacques."]
Storms are coming, storms are coming.
Come inside; come inside.
Jesus can protect us; Jesus can protect us.
Come and hide; come and hide.

Theme: Don't Be Afraid

Trouble Coming!

Just before Jesus comes back to this earth to take us home to heaven, many sad things will happen. It will be a time of trouble! Some people worry about this time—it makes them afraid. But Jesus told us we don't have to be afraid, because He will take care of us, no matter what happens.

[Sing to the tune of "Frère Jacques."]
Trouble coming, trouble coming!
Come inside; come inside.
God knows how to save us; God knows
   how to save us.

Come and hide; come and hide.

Theme: God's Word

LHFJ-18

#118

God's 10 Rules

Some people think that it is very hard to please God. They think that He has so many rules that they can't possibly follow them all. But God tried to make it very easy for us. He gave only 10 rules. We call them the Ten Commandments. When Jesus lived on earth, he followed all God's commandments. If we follow Jesus' example, we can follow all God's commandments too!

[Sing to the tune of "One Little, Two Little, Three Little Indians."]

One little, two little, three commandments;

Four little, five little, six commandments;
Seven little, eight little, nine command-
    ments—
God gave us 10 rules.

One little, two little, three rules keeping;
Four little, five little, six rules keeping;
Seven little, eight little, nine rules
    keeping—
I keep God's 10 rules.

#119

Theme: God's Word

Paul and Silas in Jail

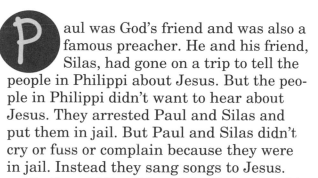
Paul was God's friend and was also a famous preacher. He and his friend, Silas, had gone on a trip to tell the people in Philippi about Jesus. But the people in Philippi didn't want to hear about Jesus. They arrested Paul and Silas and put them in jail. But Paul and Silas didn't cry or fuss or complain because they were in jail. Instead they sang songs to Jesus.

In the middle of the night God sent a big earthquake. The ground shook; the jail shook. The jailer and all the prisoners shook too. Then the walls of the jail fell down. But none of the prisoners escaped.

The jailer was so impressed that God would shake the jail down and that the prisoners didn't run away. He asked to hear more about Jesus. He and his whole family gave their hearts to Jesus and became Jesus' friends too.

[Sing to the tune of "Frère Jacques."]
Paul and Silas, Paul and Silas
Sang in jail, sang in jail.
God sent a big earthquake; God sent a
    big earthquake,
Set them free, set them free.

Theme: God's Word

#120

Devotion

Elisha and Some Naughty Boys

E lisha went from town to town in Israel, bringing them messages from God, and helping them understand how much God loved them.

Most children in the town were respectful of the prophet, but some children were not. They followed Elisha as he walked through their town, shouting mean things about his bald head. Prophet Elisha told them to go back home. But they kept following him, teasing, yelling, and making fun of his head.

Then two mother bears came out of the woods. They didn't hurt Elisha, but they chased the mean boys and hurt them.

What a sad lesson for those mean children! God wants us to be respectful. He wants us to treat our mommy and daddy and other people with respect, especially those He has called to speak for Him.

[Sing to the tune of "We Wish You a Merry Christmas."]

God wants us to be respectful;
God wants us to be respectful;
God wants us to be respectful
And treat others well.

#121

Theme: God's Word

Love My Brother/Sister

When Jesus was a little boy, He was always kind and helpful to His mommy and daddy. He played nicely with his brothers and sisters and with his friends. He was not mean to other children or to animals. God wants us to be just like Jesus was when He was a child.

[Sing to the tune of "We Wish You a Merry Christmas." Fill in the blank with brother, sister, neighbor, cousin, etc.]

God wants me to love my _____,
God wants me to love my _____,
God wants me to love my _____,

and play with them nice.

Theme: Be Kind

#122

Captain Naaman

Materials: *a sheet of blue paper or fabric, scissors, a Popsicle stick, markers*

N aaman, captain of the army of Syria, had leprosy. He came all the way to Israel to see the prophet Elijah. He asked, "Can your God help heal me?"

Elijah told him to dip seven times in the river Jordan. But Naaman went to the river and dipped six times. His spots were still there. But after the seventh dip Naaman's spots were gone! He was so happy and excited! He promised to worship the God of Israel the rest of his life.

[*Sing to the tune of "She'll Be Comin'*

'Round the Mountain."]

God said, "Dip, dip in the river to get well," etc.

Naaman dipped, dipped in the river to get well, etc.

[*Cut a slit in the blue paper (river Jordan). Draw a face on each side of the Popsicle stick. Put red polka dots on one of the faces for sick Naaman. Place the stick behind the paper and poke it up through the slit. When sick Naaman has dipped seven times, turn the stick over to show healthy Naaman.]*

Theme: God's Word

Bathe Like Naaman

Materials: *finger paint or liquid soap, red food coloring*

Remember the story of Naaman? He had the dreaded disease of leprosy. But God healed him! *[Review with your child the story of Naaman washing in the Jordan River.]*

[Use finger paint or liquid soap with a little red food coloring in it to make leprosy dots all over your child's arms and legs and tummy. Then have child dip seven times in the bathtub and wash the spots all off.]

Remember, Naaman was not healed because the river Jordan was special. Naaman was healed because he obeyed God and did exactly what God told him to do.

Theme: God's Word

#124

Everyone Will See Him

The Bible tells us many things about what will happen when Jesus comes to take us to heaven. The Bible says that His coming will not be a secret. It says that everyone will see Him when He comes. So if somebody tells you that Jesus has already come and that He is in another country, don't believe them. Jesus says everyone will see Him when He comes.

[Sing to the tune of "She'll Be Comin' 'Round the Mountain."]

God said every eye will see Him when
   He comes.

God said every eye will see Him when
   He comes.
God said every eye will see Him,
God said every eye will see Him,
God said every eye will see Him when
   He comes.

#125

Theme: God's Word

He Will Come With Lots of Angels

The Bible tells us many things that will happen when Jesus comes again. It says that Jesus will come in clouds with lots and lots of angels. It also says that we will all fly up to meet Him. Jesus isn't going to land on the ground. We are going to fly through the air and be with Jesus. We can't fly now, but when Jesus comes we will. That's because Jesus can do anything, and He will be here to take us home.

[Sing to the tune of "She'll Be Comin' 'Round the Mountain."]

He will come with lots of angels when
  He comes.
He will come with lots of angels when
  He comes.
He will come with lots of angels,
He will come with lots of angels,
He will come with lots of angels when
  He comes.

We will all rise up to meet Him when
  He comes, etc.

Theme: God's Word

LHFJ-19

#126

We'll Get Brand-new Bodies

Grandma was sick. She had cancer. The medicine she took in the hospital made all her hair fall out. It made Donnie sad to see Grandma feeling so miserable. One of the things Jesus promised us was that He would give us all brand-new bodies when He comes. Do you know someone who needs a new body, or who needs a new body part? Jesus will take care of that when He comes. Have you had trouble with your body? Jesus will take care of that too.

[Sing to the tune of "She'll Be Comin'

'Round the Mountain."]

> He will give us brand-new bodies when He comes.
> He will give us brand-new bodies when He comes.
> He will give us brand-new bodies,
> He will give us brand-new bodies,
> He will give us brand-new bodies when He comes.

#127

Theme: God's Word

We Will All Go Home With Jesus

The Bible tells us that someday the world will be destroyed because of all the bad things and the bad people in it. But we don't have to be afraid of that if we love Jesus. He promised to take us far away to heaven before He destroys the world. And later He will create our earth all over again—beautiful and perfect, as it was for Adam and Eve.

[Sing to the tune of "She'll Be Comin' 'Round the Mountain."]

We will all go home with Jesus when
   He comes.

We will all go home with Jesus when
   He comes.
We will all go home with Jesus,
We will all go home with Jesus,
We will all go home with Jesus when
   He comes.

He will take us all to heaven when He
   comes, etc.

Theme: God's Word

#128

The Golden Calf

Something very sad happened to the children of Israel right after God led them across the Red Sea. God told Moses to come talk to Him on top of Mount Sinai. While Moses was gone, the people changed their minds about following God. Instead, they made a statue of a calf out of gold. They danced around it and offered sacrifices to it and said their calf god had led them out of Egypt.

This made God very, very sad. It hurt His feelings that His people forgot all about Him and didn't love Him anymore.

When Moses came down from the mountain and saw what the people were doing, he shouted, "You need to choose right now! If you're on God's side, stand over here. If the calf is your god, go stand over there."

Everyone had to make a choice.

God lets you make a choice too. God is very happy when we choose His side, because He loves us so much.

[Sing to the tune of "She'll Be Comin' 'Round the Mountain."]

If you want to be on God's side, clap your hands (etc.).

#129

Theme: God's Word

Be Like Jesus

Jesus came to earth as a baby, then grew into a little boy. He had to learn to play with others and get along with His brothers and sisters, just as we do. Jesus was our example so that we would know just how God wants us to act. He wants us to play nicely with our brothers and sisters and to be kind to our pets and our friends. But it's always our choice. Every day we can choose to act like Jesus.

[Sing to the tune of "She'll Be Comin' 'Round the Mountain."]

If you want to be like Jesus, clap your hands.
If you want to be like Jesus, clap your hands.
If you want to be like Jesus,
If you want to be like Jesus,
If you want to be like Jesus, clap your hands.
Jesus can hear you clapping. He knows which choice you made. He loves you, and He will always help you when you choose Him.

Theme: Learning to Play Together

#130

Just Say No!

S atan is God's enemy. He's not as strong as God, but he tries very hard to hurt God by hurting God's friends or making them not care about God anymore. Satan encourages us to do things that God doesn't like. We call this being tempted.

Sometimes Satan puts ideas into our minds that can get us into trouble. Other times he makes bad things happen to make us angry or sad.

We need to learn to say No to Satan. Satan even tempted Jesus when He lived here, but Jesus always said No!

[Sing to the tune of "She'll Be Comin' 'Round the Mountain."]

When Satan tries to tempt you, just say No *[stamp foot and shout, "No! No!"]*
When Satan tries to tempt you, just say No *["No! No!"]*
When Satan tries to tempt you,
When Satan tries to tempt you,
When Satan tries to tempt you, just say No *["No! No!"].*

#131

Theme: Temptation

Lots of Fresh Air

J esus made our bodies just perfect. And He gives us everything we need to keep them working just right. That way we will be healthy and happy. Our bodies work best with lots of fresh air. We need to take big breaths of fresh air every day to keep our bodies healthy.

[Sing to the tune of "Here We Go 'Round the Mulberry Bush."]

Lots of fresh air is good for me,
Good for me, good for me.
Lots of fresh air is good for me.
It makes my body healthy.

Theme: Healthy Body

#132

My Nose, Throat, and Lungs

One of the most important things our bodies need is in the air. It is called oxygen. In order for you to get the oxygen out of the air, Jesus made a hole in your face and covered it with your nose. Then He made a tube that starts at your nose and goes down your throat and into your chest. At the end of the tube He put two big pink things that look like balloons. They are called lungs. Your lungs take oxygen out of the air. All the leftovers get blown back up the tube and out your nose when you breathe out.

[Do the actions to this finger play together.]
Jesus made my nose *[point to nose]*
    to breathe in clean, fresh air
    [inhale deeply].
Jesus made my throat to go from here
    [point to nose] to there *[point
    to chest].*
Jesus made my lungs to blow the bad
    air out *[blow].*
Isn't He a wonderful Jesus! *[Clap and
    cheer for Jesus.]*

#133

Theme: Healthy Body

Rest

After playing and working hard all day, we need rest. To make sure we get enough rest, God made our world so that part of the time it is light, and part of the time it is dark. When it's light, we can play and do our work. When it's dark, it's time to rest.

God wants us to get enough rest to keep our bodies healthy. But He doesn't sleep— He watches over us all night long and wakes us up in the morning.

[Sing to the tune of "Taps." Sing softly and slowly as a lullaby.]

Theme: Healthy Body

LHFJ-20

Day is done. Good night, sun! Good night, sky!
Hello, stars! Hello, moon!
Close your eyes; safely rest.
God loves you.

#134

Boaz

Materials: *a seed, potting soil, a small container*

The Bible tells a story about a man named Boaz. Boaz was a good, kind man. Boaz was a farmer. He and his helpers planted lots of seeds to grow things for people to eat.

We are going to plant a seed and pretend to be like Boaz. Boaz made sure he had good ground to plant the seeds in. He didn't plant his seeds in rocky places or the desert. He planted his seeds where there was good, fertile soil.

We're going to put some soil in this container. Now poke a hole with your finger and drop the seed in. Cover it up. When Boaz planted the seed, he prayed and asked God to take care of his plants and to water them for him.

Does God send angels with watering cans to water the outside plants? No! He sends the rain. But since this seed is an inside plant, we will have to make sure it gets water. *[Help your child water the seed.]* Give your seed just a little bit of water every day and watch for it to grow. Farmers like Boaz have to be patient, because it takes many days for a seed to grow.

Theme: Nature

Seed Fun

Materials: *a clear glass jar, paper towels, and some seeds*

When farmer Boaz planted seeds in the ground, he couldn't see what was happening until the little green plants poked up through the dirt. But I think you would like to see what happens before they poke through the dirt, wouldn't you?

[Presoak the seeds in water overnight. Let child arrange seeds on a wet paper towel. Then slide it into a glass jar so that the seeds are visible from the outside. Crumple wet paper towels inside the jar and loosely cover its mouth. Dampen the paper towels again in the evening. In a day or two you should have little sprouts coming from the seeds. After the seeds sprout, poke holes in potting soil and drop them in so they can make their roots under the ground.]

Theme: Nature

#136

Footprints

Sometimes people talk about following in Jesus' footsteps. Since Jesus doesn't live on earth anymore, He can't leave actual footprints for us to see. But by learning about Jesus from the Bible, we can follow in His footsteps by acting like Him. I want to follow in Jesus' footprints, don't you?

[Go to a muddy or sandy place where footprints can be easily seen. Point out any footprints or tracks in the sand or mud. Explain how we can tell what kind of animal has been there by the prints they leave.

Press two fingers into the dirt and show the kind of track that deer hooves make. Then have child press his/her foot into the dirt. Say, "That's your footprint." Press your footprint next to child's, then walk away and say, "Would you be able to follow me by looking at my footprints—even if you couldn't see me?" Help child follow your footprints.]

#137

Theme: Be Like Jesus

Animal Motions

 elp child do the actions for this activity.]
 Fish swim. *[Child lies on floor, legs together, holding arms to body, and wiggles like a fish.]*
 Snakes slither. *[Child keeps arms close to body and slithers like a snake.]*
 Bugs crawl. *[Child crawls on hands and knees.]*
 Bunnies hop. *[Child stands upright and hops.]*
 Birds fly. *[Child flaps arms like wings.]*
 And people walk. *[Child walks.]*

Theme: Nature

[Have child lie back down on the floor.]
 God made fish just right for swimming. *[Swimming motion.]* God made snakes just right for slithering. *[Slithering motion.]* God made bugs just right for crawling. *[Crawl.]* God made bunnies just right for hopping. *[Hop.]* God made birds just right for flying. *[Flap arms.]* And God made people just right for walking. *[Walk.]*
 God is so wise. Thank You, God!

#138

Reminders of God's Love

Materials: *a baby food jar with lid, light glue, artificial flowers*

God made the flowers to show us how much He loves us. Different flowers bloom at different times, but none of them last very long. Today we are going to make a flower reminder to remind us that even when there aren't any flowers outside, we can see that God loves us.

[Have child glue an artificial flower on the inside of the baby food jar lid. This is best done with a flower that will fill part of the jar (such as a rose), rather than a flat one (such as a daisy). Carefully fit the jar over the flower. Place glue around the rim of the jar and press firmly into lid. Optional: cut a circle of green fabric and have child cut fringe edging on it with scissors. Place upside-down baby food jar in the middle of the fabric circle and tie a ribbon around lid so that flower appears to be growing in grass. Use for a paperweight.]

Dear Jesus, every time I see my flower reminder, please help me to remember how much You love me. I love You too. Amen.

#139

Theme: Nature

My Kidneys, Part 1

D
e
v
o
t
i
o
n

Materials: *a funnel, coffee filter or paper towel, water, red food coloring, sand or dirt*

To keep our bodies healthy, we need lots of water. Do you know why? We have lots of blood inside our bodies. And blood is mostly water!

Blood goes everywhere in our bodies. It gets oxygen in our lungs and takes it to every part of our bodies. The blood takes food in tiny pieces from our stomachs and carries it all through our bodies. We have two filters in our bodies that keep our blood clean. These filters are called kidneys.

[Make a kidney by putting a coffee filter or folded paper towel in a funnel. Mix water and red food coloring to make "blood." Stir sand into the blood and pour it through the filter.]

See how the filter catches the sand, but lets the clean "blood" flow through the funnel into the glass?

Theme: Healthy Body

#140

My Kidneys, Part 2

Materials: *kidney filter from devotion 140, cornstarch*

Bring some water to a boil while mixing 2 tablespoons of cornstarch in ¼ cup of cold water. Add boiling water to the cornstarch mixture, stirring rapidly. Aim for a gravy consistency. Add red food coloring to make mixture look like blood.]

Drinking water is important for our kidney filters. Watch what happens when we pour thick blood into the kidney filter. *[Pour mixture into filter. Very little fluid will pour through. Allow child to pour six glasses of water slowly, one by one, into the filter.]*

See how much better the filter works now, and how the "blood" pours through into the glass? Our kidney filters work much better, too, when we drink enough water. To take care of our bodies, we must drink water every day so that our kidney filters will work properly and not get clogged up.

#141

Theme: Healthy Body

Bath Time

We have learned that water is very good for the insides of our bodies, but did you know that water is good for our outsides, too? That is why we take a bath! Bathing helps keep our skin nice and clean. If we never took a bath, we would get sore and very dirty. (And after a while we would smell bad, too!)

Jesus wants us to take care of the inside *and* the outside of our bodies. This is why we take a bath. This means we are pleasing Jesus, even when we're taking a bath in the bathtub.

Go take a bath!

Thank You, Jesus, for showing us how to keep our bodies healthy and how to take care of them, and how to please You, too. Amen.

Theme: Healthy Body

LHFJ-21

#142

Sunshine

Thank You, God, for the sunshine.

I like sunny days, don't you? Sunny days are good days for playing outside. Not only is sunlight pretty and makes good weather; it is also good for our bodies. Jesus put something special inside your skin that makes your body able to make vitamin D out of sunshine. This means that every time you go outside to play, if any of your skin is showing—even just your hands and face—it is helping your body make vitamins and get strong and healthy.

Take your child out to play and make some vitamin D.

#143

Theme: Healthy Body

Be Careful With Sunshine!

Although sunshine is good for our bodies, too much is a bad thing. If you spend too much time out in the hot sun in the middle of the day, it can hurt your skin. Your skin can become very red and it hurts! We call this sunburn.

Jesus wants us to take care of the inside and the outside of our body. It makes Him sad if we hurt. It is wise not to spend too much time out in the sun in the middle of the day when your skin could burn. If you are going to be outside during that time, ask Mom to put sunblock lotion on your skin.

[Give child a small amount of sunblock lotion in the palm of each hand. Help him/her rub it on arms and exposed skin. If sunblock is not appropriate on this day, use a dab of regular moisturizing lotion.]

Dear Jesus, help me remember to take good care of my skin. Amen.

Theme: Healthy Body

#144

Going With Jesus

Materials: *small Fisher Price characters (or make your own out of Popsicle sticks or pipe cleaners)*

I n a sandbox, help child build a little town with houses, populated with "people." It can be very simple or very complex, using little cars and twigs for trees, etc.]

The Bible tells us that someday the world is going to be destroyed because of all the bad things that are happening in it. We don't have to be afraid, because Jesus is going to take us away before the world is destroyed. *[Take all the people out and set them to the side in a safe place. Then use a rake to smooth the whole sandbox.]*

Jesus has made another promise that is very exciting. Jesus has promised to make our earth all brand-new and perfect. *[Help child build new houses, new twigs for trees, new roads, etc.]*

Let's bring the people back from the safe place and set them all in the new earth. Jesus told us everything that is going to happen so we would never have to be scared. And it will be exciting to see Him create a whole, new world for us.

Thank You, Jesus, for telling us everything You plan to do to take care of us when the world is destroyed. Amen.

#145

Theme: God's Word

Morning

Materials: *poster board, scissors, string, paper clip*

H ave child draw and color a large sun, preferably on heavy paper or poster board. Cut it out. Punch a hole in the top and thread a string through, or attach a paper clip to thread a string through if it is made of lighter paper. Laying the sun flat on the floor, loop the middle of the string up over a doorknob, a curtain rod, or a cupboard handle, and give the other end of the string to the child.]

When God created our world, He created daytime and nighttime. Then He made lights for the daytime, and lights for the nighttime. *[Have child pull the string until the sun comes up.]* We call this sunrise.

In some parts of the world you have to get up very early for sunrise. In other places the sun rises the same time every day. But every day there is a sunrise.

God gave us the sun to light our day, to help make the earth nice and warm, and to help our bodies make vitamin D. The sun helps the grass and the plants grow, too. *[Have child make the sun rise several times.]*

Thank You, God, for making the sun rise every day.

Theme: Nature

#146

Sunset

Materials: *sun on string from sunrise activity in devotional 146*

ach time you say "sunset," have the child lower the sun down until it lays flat on the floor.]

When Jesus made our world, He divided each day into two parts: the night and the day. The Bible says that the evening and the morning were the first day. That means that each new day starts in the evening. We can tell it's evening when the sun seems to go down behind the hills *[or the horizon if you live in a place without hills].* When the sun goes down, we call that sunset.

We like to watch the sunset. The sky makes lots of beautiful colors—and then it gets dark. The sunset is the beginning of the new day, and we go to bed and rest.

This is an especially important time every Friday. When the sun goes down on Friday, it is the beginning of Sabbath. That's our rest day. It is our family day, too, because our parents don't have to go to work, and we can all be together.

Because of the sunset, we can always tell when a new day is beginning. I'm glad God made sunset!

Thank you, God, for sunset! Amen.

#147

Theme: Nature

Jesus Our Healer

Materials: *small bowl of ketchup*

 his activity is best done in the bathtub.]
   When Jesus was here on earth, He healed many people who came to Him with problems. Some people had sores on their body. *[Dip your finger in the ketchup and make little ketchup dots on child's arms or legs.]* Some had big cuts where they had been hurt. *[Dip your finger in the ketchup and draw a line on child's arms or legs.]* Jesus was able to heal them and make all their hurts go away. *[Wipe a washcloth over the child's "injuries" and* *make them disappear.]*
   When Jesus healed the people while He was here on this earth, they were well right away. Jesus created our bodies so that they heal a little bit slower, but it works too. If you get a skinned knee *[smear ketchup on child's knee]* it doesn't stay skinned forever. In a few days it is all better. How kind of Jesus to think ahead and make our bodies this way! *[Wipe washcloth over child and wipe away all "wounds."]*
   Thank You, Jesus, for being such a good healer. Amen.

Theme: Healthy Body

#148

Broken Bones

Materials: *a small ace bandage (or make your own by cutting a long, narrow strip of material and roll up tightly)*

Jesus knew that sometimes even very strong bones could break. So He made our bodies with strong, stretchy muscles around our bones, and skin on top of the muscles to hold everything together. So even when the bone inside your leg gets broken, the strong stretchy muscles and the skin help hold everything together until your bone heals.

The doctor uses a special bandage, something like this, to wrap up the leg carefully. *[Wrap the ace bandage snugly around child's leg but not tight enough to impede circulation.]* The bandage becomes very hard—we call the hard bandage a cast—and it holds the leg straight and in the correct position until the bone can heal.

But doctors can't make bones heal—only Jesus can do that. He made our bodies so that the food we eat soaks into our bones and makes them strong again. Then we don't need the cast any longer. *[Take off the ace bandage from child.]*

Thank You, Jesus, for making our bones able to heal and get better. You are so wise and wonderful! Amen.

#149

Theme: Healthy Body

God's Promise to Abraham

Materials: *black construction paper, gum stars*

A braham did not have any children. He was old enough to be a grandpa. His wife, Sarah, was old enough to be a grandma, and still God had not given them any babies of their own.

One night Abraham was praying. God said, "Abraham, look up at the stars. Can you count them?"

"No," said Abraham. "There are too many to count."

God said, "That's how many children and grandchildren and great-great-great grand-children you will have. Your family will have so many people in it that there will be as many of them as there are stars in the sky!"

Abraham knew God always keeps His promises. Today there are thousands and thousands of Jewish people—all of them are part of Abraham's family. God kept His promise!

[See how many gum stars child can put on black construction paper without letting any of the stars touch. The younger the child is, the smaller the paper needs to be so that child can finish the activity without becoming bored. Hang the star picture in his/her room as a reminder God always keeps His promises.]

Theme: God's Word

#150

Isaac's Kind Wife

I saac needed a wife. But the women who lived near Isaac didn't worship God. Isaac wanted a wife who loved God as much as he did. So Isaac's father, Abraham, sent his servant, Eliezer, back to the country where people worshiped God to find a wife for Isaac.

Eliezer wanted to find Isaac a good wife who was kind. When he arrived, he stopped at the well where people came to get their water. He asked, "Could I have a drink of water?"

A very pretty girl was kind and got him a drink. First, she had to tie a rope on her jug, then lower it down, down, down into the well and scoop up the water. Then she had to pull, pull, pull the jug all the way back up. She gave Eliezer a drink, and then she got drinks for all his camels. And camels drink lots and lots of water!

"This is the one," said Eliezer.

Her name was Rebekah. She traveled back with Eliezer and became Isaac's wife.

It is being kind to offer drinks of water to thirsty people. Let's get some water right now. I will go get a drink for you, and you can get a drink for me and for our pets.

#151

Theme: God's Word

Jacob's Ladder

Materials: *several drinking straws, a piece of construction paper*

J acob played a trick on his brother, Esau, that Esau didn't like at all. Jacob had to run away from home so Esau wouldn't hurt him. He felt very sad. He wondered if God still loved him and was still looking after him. *[Ask your child, "Do you think God still loved him?"]* Yes, God always loves us—even when we are in trouble or have done something wrong.

When night came, Jacob had no bed to sleep in. He had to lie on the hard ground. He felt very lonely. While he was sleeping, he had a dream. He dreamed he saw a big ladder that went all the way up to heaven. Angels went up and down on the ladder. When Jacob woke up, he knew God was sending angels to watch over him.

God loves you, too, even when you have done something wrong.

[Help child make a picture of Jacob's ladder. Glue two straws on the paper, then allow child to cut other straws into shorter lengths and glue them as cross pieces to the ladder. Allow it to dry, then hang in child's room as a reminder that God looks after us even when we have been in trouble.]

Theme: God's Word

#152

Baby Moses

Materials: *construction paper, green yarn*

*U*se one sheet of light-blue paper for the background of picture. Fold a second sheet of paper in half and cut an oval basket-shape, making sure the fold serves as one side of the basket. Out of lighter paper, cut a circle for the baby's head and a large contrasting oval for his body. Explain that baby is wrapped in a blanket. Unfold oval basket-piece. Allow child to glue head and body in the basket. Draw a smiley face on the head, then close the basket. Draw river on the large background sheet and have child glue several lengths of green yarn for the bulrushes.

Then glue the basket to the river. Now child can open basket to check on the baby.]

When Baby Moses was born, the pharaoh made a horrible rule: all baby boys had to be thrown in the river! Baby Moses' mother put him in the river in a little basket boat so he would be safe. Then she sent his big sister, Miriam, to stay near and watch over him. *[Help child open basket to peek at the baby.]*

Somebody still checks on you all the time to make sure you are OK, too. I'm so glad God gave every baby somebody to watch over him or her, aren't you?

Theme: God's Word

The Burning Bush, Part 1

Materials: *paper, crayons or markers, a piece of clear, acrylic sheeting, such as overhead transparency or report cover*

Moses lived out in the desert taking care of sheep. He had been out there a long time and had seen everything that was there several times, but one day he saw something new. He saw a little bush that was on fire. He had seen bushes on fire before, but this one stayed bright and green *and didn't burn up!* He hadn't seen *that* before.

Usually when a bush is burning it gets all burned up and turns into ashes. But this was a special bush. Moses came closer to look. Then God spoke to him from the bush.

God chooses special ways to talk to people so they will be interested and listen. I'm glad God does that, aren't you?

[Have child color a green bush on the background paper. Draw flames on the acrylic overhead and place over the bush. This way, child can pick up the acrylic and still look underneath and see that the bush is staying nice and green and not burning up. If you have smearing problems cut flames from orange construction paper and glue on acetate page.]

Thank You, God, for finding special ways to talk to people so that they listen. Amen.

Theme: God's Word

#154

The Burning Bush, Part 2

Moses was taking care of his sheep when he saw a strange sight: a bush was burning, but it stayed green and did not get burned up. Moses was very surprised and went over to check it out. God was in the bush, and He told Moses, "Take off your shoes, because where you are standing is holy ground." *[Have child take off shoes.]*

Where Moses lived, taking off your shoes was a sign of respect. God wants us to respect any place where He is. That's why we're reverent and respectful in church.

Where we live, we don't take off our shoes to show respect, but we can be quiet and walk softly and talk softly and not run or play in God's house. This is how we show respect.

Dear God, help me always to show respect for You. Amen.

#155

Theme: God's Word

Spitting

Materials: *a small hollow rubber ball or a squeaky toy*

**D**raw *a face on the rubber ball with a permanent marker. Poke a hole in the mouth you have drawn. Place under water and squeeze to fill.]*

Spitting is something we can do with our mouth. *[Squeeze the toy to make a little water shoot out.]* There are good times and bad times for spitting. Good times would be when you've chewed something that tastes bad. Then we always spit in a napkin or paper towel. We spit in the sink when we brush our teeth, too.

Bad times for spitting are inside the house, on the floor, or on furniture. We should not spit on people, either. Spitting on people is mean, and it hurts their feelings.

[Refill the rubber ball toy and give to the child. Provide a paper towel.] Listen to what I say, and if it is a good time to spit, make the toy spit. But if it's a bad time to spit, say "No!"

Is it OK to spit on the floor? in the sink while I'm brushing my teeth? on sombody I don't like? into a napkin or paper towel? on a friend?

Dear Jesus, help me to remember to spit only at the right times. Amen.

Theme: Good Manners

#156

Devotion

Jesus Made My Mouth, Part 1

Materials: *a small paper plate*

old paper plate in half. Make "lips" on the border edge and a "tongue" inside the paper plate. Place plate in your child's hand, folded edge against the palm. Tape fingers to the top side and thumb to the bottom side, so that by opening and closing hand, the paper plate mouth opens and closes.]

Jesus gave us each a mouth. But we have to be careful with the teeth in our mouth and use them to bite only right things. Our teeth in our mouth are for biting things that are good to eat. *[Have several items the child can select.]*

Is it OK to bite a banana? a slice of bread? a doll? a block? a pencil? a pillow? *[Put object up to the paper-plate mouth. If it's OK, have child use the mouth to bite object. If not, have child say "No!" Repeat this activity with several items.]*

Jesus wants us to be careful what we bite. We *never* bite people or pets. Biting hurts. Jesus wants us to be kind to our family, our friends, and our pets.

Dear Jesus, please help me to be wise and know which things to bite and which things not to. I want to be kind like you. Amen.

#157

Theme: Respect

Jesus Made My Mouth, Part 2

Materials: *paper plate mouth from devotion 157*

hen Jesus made our mouths, He was very clever. He made them so we are able to do many things. Because of our mouths, we can eat and they can bite. We can spit and we can talk. Jesus wants us to use our mouths to say only good things. *[Help child open and close paper-plate mouth to pretend to talk. Make a paper-plate mouth for your hand too. Have child's paper-plate mouth repeat after you.]*

Here are nice things we can say: please, thank you, and I love you. Jesus never wants us to say mean things that will hurt other people's feelings. *[Help child repeat after you, saying nice things with their mouth.]*

Dear Jesus, thank You for teaching us how to be kind to each other. Help me to use my mouth to say only kind things. Amen.

Theme: Respect

#158

A Bed for Baby Jesus

Materials: *small box, yellow yarn cut into three- to six-inch lengths*

When Baby Jesus was born, His mommy and daddy were on a trip. They had gone to a town named Bethlehem. When they got there, so many people had also come that there was no room in the inn. They had to sleep out with the animals. Jesus' mother made a bed for Him in a box that was filled with hay for the animals to eat. She wrapped Jesus in a special cloth so that the hay wouldn't make His skin itchy.

When you were born, we had a special bed for you to sleep in, and you have a bed now. But Jesus had to sleep in a box of hay near the animals. How much Jesus must have loved us to be willing to come to this earth. He knew that He would be coming to a poor family who was on a trip and that He wouldn't even have a bed to sleep in His first night. He came anyway because He loves you and me and other people. What a wonderful God we have!

We will fill this box with "hay" and pretend it is the box that Jesus slept in when He was born. Every time we look at the box it will help us remember how much Jesus loves us.

#159

Theme: God's Word

The Yuckiest Job

Materials: *small basin of water*

s you tell the story, wash the child's feet in the basin and dry them with a towel.]

In families, everybody has a job. Daddy's job is _____ . Mommy's job is _____. And _____ takes care of you. *[Fill in the blanks with Mommy and Daddy and the names of any other people involved with your child's care.]*

There are lots of small jobs to do, too. Somebody has to cook supper, empty wastebaskets, pick up toys, and wash the dishes.

There is always a job we really don't like to do. When Jesus was here, the yuckiest job was washing people's feet. When they came in the house, somebody brought a basin and washed everybody's feet so they wouldn't bring dirt into the house.

When Jesus and His friends got together for dinner one night, nobody wanted the yuckiest job. So Jesus got the water and started washing their feet. Everyone felt bad since He was the most important person there. Jesus did this to show us that we should be willing to do even the yuckiest job for other people, because we love them.

Theme: God's Word

#160

The Widow's Offering

Materials: *several coins, a metal pie plate (or other container that will be noisy when coins are dropped in it)*

Two people gave their offerings at church. One was a very rich man. *[Give your child several coins.]* He held his money up high and dropped it noisily into the offering plate so that everyone could see how much he was giving. *[Have child hold money high and drop it noisily into the offering plate.]*

A woman was at church that day too. Her husband had died, and she was very poor. Even so, she brought two pennies to give to God. *[Give child two pennies.]* The poor woman put her pennies in very quietly.

[Have child pretend he/she is the poor woman and put pennies into the dish quietly.] She was embarrassed because she didn't have very much money to give.

Jesus told His friends that the poor woman had actually given a bigger offering than the rich man because the rich man still had lots of money left. The poor woman had given all the money she had. Jesus appreciates when we give Him gifts. No gift is too small to give Jesus. He understands when people don't have very much. Jesus loves poor people as much as He loves rich people.

#161

Theme: God's Word

Peter in Prison

Materials: *six-inch strips of paper, glue or tape*

Help child glue or tape the ends of paper strips together to make a chain. Fasten chain around child's wrists and ankles.]

Peter was one of Jesus' disciples. After Jesus went back to heaven, Peter became a missionary and went everywhere telling people the story of Jesus. One day some Roman soldiers arrested Peter. They took him to prison and put chains on him and put him in a little cell with a guard to watch him.

"Now, you can't tell anyone else about Jesus," the soldiers said.

But during the night, an angel came. He opened the prison door and told Peter, "Come with me!"

Peter stood up. His chains fell off, and he went with the angel. *[Have child break the chains and "escape."]*

God can even rescue people from prison. Our God is so strong He can do anything!

Theme: God's Word

Devotion

Paul and Silas

Materials: *wet wash cloth*

Paul and Silas loved Jesus and traveled to many places, telling people about how much Jesus loved them. In one town they were arrested for telling people about Jesus. The people pulled the missionaries' shirts off and hit them again and again. Then they were locked up in jail.

During the night God sent an earthquake, and Paul and Silas were set free. The jailer realized that God was more powerful than his jail and that these people were God's friends. "Please forgive me," he said, "for being so mean to you. I want to love Jesus too."

Paul and Silas forgave the jailer and taught him all about Jesus. Then the jailer brought them to his house. He washed their sore backs with a cold wet cloth and made them feel so much better. *[Use the cool wet washcloth to wipe your child's hands and face—and back, if it is convenient.]*

Jesus wants us to forgive people who have been mean to us, too. Sometimes that's hard to do.

Dear Jesus, help me to forgive people who have been mean to me, just as Paul and Silas forgave. Amen.

#163

Theme: God's Word

Daniel's Brave Friends, Part 1

Materials: *tape recorder or radio*

D aniel and his friends had grown up in Israel, and their Jewish parents believed in God. Then they were taken as prisoners to Babylon, where everyone worshiped idols.

The king built a big statue. He put it in a place where everyone in the city could be invited. He told the people, "When you hear the music play, bow down and pray to the statue."

Daniel's friends said to each other, "We can't pray to this idol! What are we going to do?"

The king had a big furnace built. He said, "Anyone who does not pray to the statue will get thrown in the fiery furnace."

Then the music started. Everyone knelt down, except Daniel's friends.

"Maybe you didn't understand," said the king. "I know you're Daniel's friends, and I don't want to do anything bad to you. Now, we'll do this again, and when the music plays, you must kneel down." *[Use a tape recorder to play music. Have child be one of Daniel's friends.]* The music played again.

"Kneel down!" shouted the king.

Did Daniel's friends kneel down and pray to the statue? No, they didn't!

Theme: God's Word

#164

Daniel's Brave Friends, Part 2

T he king had made a great statue. He invited all the people to come. When the music played, everyone was supposed to kneel down and worship the statue or they would be thrown into the fiery furnace. But Daniel's friends did not kneel down when the music played.

The king's guards carried them over to the fiery furnace and put them in. *[Pick up child, carry him/her to couch, and put down.]* It was so hot that the guards fell down. But Daniel's friends just stood there. The fire didn't burn them up.

The king looked into the furnace. Then he looked again. His guards had put the three friends into the furnace, but the king saw *four* people in there! Jesus was there in the fiery furnace with the three friends, and they were safe. They did not get burned.

The king called them to come out. Daniel's friends were faithful to God, and God was faithful to them. They didn't get hurt. The king was so impressed that he knelt down and worshiped God too.

Our God is the strongest, most powerful God. We should worship only Him.

#165

Theme: God's Word

Which God Is Strongest?

Materials: *paper, tape*

Draw a square and color it gray. Draw *orange fire on the top and fold paper in half so that fire cannot be seen.]*
Elijah worshiped God. But the king and queen of Israel and most of the people worshiped an idol named Baal. This made God unhappy. And it made Elijah unhappy too, because he loved God.

One day Elijah, the king, the queen, and all the prophets of Baal met on top of a mountain for a contest. They built two altars exactly the same.

All day the priests danced around their altar and sang and shouted, but nothing happened. Baal couldn't send fire.

Then Elijah prayed to God. "Please send fire so these people will know You are the true God." *Crash!* Lightning flashed from heaven. *[Flip fire up from the back of child's picture.]* Fire burned up the sacrifice and the altar. Everybody saw that God was the most powerful. Everybody had a chance to choose again. God gives us a chance to choose Him too. I choose to worship God. How about you?

Dear Jesus, I choose to worship You. Amen.

Theme: God's Word

#166

Elijah and the Rain

Option: *[This is best done near a sink or in a bathtub.]*

Elijah worshiped God. The king and the queen worshiped an idol named Baal. They thought Baal sent rain for their gardens. Elijah told them, "Only God can send rain. God will not send any more rain until you stop worshiping Baal."

The king was angry. "Kill that man!"

But God helped Elijah escape. For three years there was no rain. The trees and the grass and the plants got brown. The gardens died. The people didn't have enough food to eat. They didn't have enough water to drink. They were thirsty all the time. The lakes and rivers dried up. The ponds dried up.

One day Elijah came to see the king. "You caused all this trouble," said the king.

"No," said Elijah, "you caused all this trouble by saying Baal makes the rain." Then Elijah asked God to send rain again. *[Turn on the faucet. Sprinkle drops of water on child.]* Soon the rivers were flowing again. The trees grew leaves. The gardens grew food. Everyone knew that God sends the rain.

Thank You, God, for sending the rain. Amen.

#167

Theme: God's Word

My Digestion

Materials: *a colander, a large bowl to put under the colander, dried beans, a dry ingredient (salt, sugar, or flour)*

esus made our bodies so we could eat many kinds of food. We chew up the food and swallow it. First it goes to our tummies; then it goes into a very long tube that curls back and forth and around and around. It soaks up only the things from our food that our bodies need to make them strong and healthy.

All the food our bodies don't need comes out the end of the tube. This is what happens when we go to the bathroom.

[Have child stir dry ingredients into the beans in a bowl. Mix it up carefully.] Food is a mixture of things our bodies need, and some things that our bodies don't need. *[Dump the mixture into the colander. Have the child shake the colander.]* The colander is like the tube in our body. See how some of the food goes into the bowl and the rest of it stays in here? Then our bodies can dump out what they don't need. *[Dump the colander contents into another bowl.]*

Jesus was so wise to make our bodies just right. He's happy when we take care of them.

Dear Jesus, thank You for making my body. You are so wise and wonderful. Amen.

Theme: Healthy Body

#168

Motor Movement

One of the most wonderful things made was your brain. Your head has a hard bone, called a skull, that protects your brain so it can't get hurt. Your brain controls everything that happens in your body.

Can you swing your hand around and around in a circle? The reason you are able to do that is that your brain sends a message to your arm and tells it to do that. Can you swing both arms? Your brain is able to send more than one message at a time. Lie on your back and wiggle both arms and one leg.

Now wiggle both arms and both legs. Jesus made our brains able to control our arms and legs. We can wiggle them, swing them around and around in circles, and kick them.

Jesus made our brains so wonderfully. He wants us to use our brains to choose what we do with our arms and legs. Jesus made our bodies to do good things. Let's choose never to do anything with our arms or legs that would hurt someone else.

Dear Jesus, thank You for making my body. Help me to only use it for good things. Amen.

Theme: Healthy Body

Temperature

Materials: *a bowl of warm water, a bowl of cold water (preferably with ice cubes)*

Jesus made your brain able to do many other things besides just wiggle your arms and legs. Your brain is also able to tell temperature. Put your hand in this first bowl. What do you feel? Now put your hand in the second bowl. Is it different? What is different?

Jesus made little nerves in your body. Nerves are little message channels that take the message from your fingers up to your brain and say, "This is what I am feeling." Then your brain says, "This water is cold," or "This water is warm." If our bodies couldn't do this, we wouldn't know when it was cold and we needed to put on a sweater, or when we were too hot and needed to go sit in the shade or get a drink of water.

Jesus was so wise and wonderful! When He made our bodies, He thought of everything we would need.

Thank You, Jesus, for making my brain and my nerves. Amen.

Theme: Healthy Body

#170

My Hearing

Materials: *cooking pot, bell, sheet of paper and other "noise" items*

Have child sit with back to you so he/she can't see what you're doing.] Jesus gave you something special to tell you what is going on around you so you can tell what's happening behind you—even though you can't see it. *[Ring bell.]* What do you hear? Yes, it's a bell. *[Tap metal spoon on cooking pan.]* What do you hear? Yes, I'm banging a spoon on a pan. *[Crumple up piece of paper.]* What do you hear? Yes, this is paper crackling.

Jesus gave us two ears so that we could hear the things that are going on around us. Jesus made our ears so special that we can hear even very quiet noises. Jesus wants us to take good care of our ears. Listening to noises that are too loud can hurt our ears. Putting things inside our ears can hurt them too.

Jesus gave us such special gifts. *[Touch child's ears.]* And we need to take good care of them.

Dear Jesus, thank You for giving me my ears. Please help me to take good care of them. Amen.

#171

Theme: Healthy Body

Plants Need Sunshine, Part 1

Materials: *a plant with large leaves, dark construction paper, tape [Fold construction paper and tape so that it covers half of a leaf.]*

W e are going to cover up part of this leaf, and then we are going to put our plant where it can get sunlight. It can get sunlight in a window or in any room that has sunshine. Or we could put it outside. We're going to watch and find out what happens to the part of the leaf that doesn't get any sunshine.

Dear Jesus, we are doing this experiment to find out more about the way You made plants and how they need sunshine. Thank You for making plants and sunshine. Amen.

[Allow the covering to stay on leaf for at least two days. Then remove the paper covering without damaging the leaf. One half of the leaf should be a much lighter color—it even may be yellow.]

[Two days later:] See how the leaf stayed nice and green on the part the sunshine could shine on? But the part that couldn't get any sunshine lost its color and doesn't look as healthy. Plants need sunshine. It helps them grow. You need sunshine too.

Thank You, Jesus, for making sunshine so the plants and trees can grow. Amen.

Theme: Nature

#172

Devotion

Plants Need Sunshine, Part 2

Materials: *houseplant*

All plants need sunshine. Let's put this plant near a window and see what happens.

Dear Jesus, we want to learn more about how You made plants and sunshine work together. Amen.

[Check plant the next day. The leaves should be curling toward the window.]

Now let's try something new. Let's turn the plant so that all the leaves that were pointing *toward* the window are now pointing *away* from the window.

[Check the plant again in a few days. The leaves will have turned toward the light.]

The plant needs the light to grow. Jesus is our light, and we need to turn toward Him to grow too. A plant turns toward the sun, wherever the sun is. We turn toward Jesus when we close our eyes and talk to Him. We can turn to Jesus, no matter where we are and no matter which direction we are facing. Let's close our eyes and turn to Jesus right now.

Thank You, Jesus, for making light so my plants can grow. Help me to turn to You just as my plant turns toward the sunshine. Amen.

#173

Theme: Nature

My Eyes

Materials: *mirror, bright light*

Look at your eyes in the mirror. Aren't they beautiful? Jesus made our eyes so we can see things. He made our eyes so that we can see things in bright light, and so we see things when light isn't so bright.

See the very middle part of your eye? It is black. The part around it is colored. Watch what happens when your eye sees more light. *[Turn on a very bright light. Do not shine it directly in child's eyes.]* Watch what happens to the black part of your eye. See? It gets very tiny.

[Take the bright light away.] Now watch what happens. The black part of your eye gets tiny when the light is bright, so the light can't hurt your eyes. It gets bigger when there is less light, so you can still see well.

Isn't Jesus wonderful? He made our eyes to be able to change according to how much light we have.

Thank You, Jesus, for making my eyes so special. Amen.

Theme: Healthy Body

LHFJ-25

#174

My Larynx

Take your child's hand and place it on the front of your throat.] Can you feel a big bump in my neck? This is called a larynx. It's a special place God made in my throat so I would be able to talk.

Now put your hand on the front of *your* neck. Can you find *your* larynx? What happens when you swallow? *[If your child can't find larynx, allow him/her to put hand on your throat, then drink several swallows of water.]* What happens? That's right! The larynx bobs up and down when you swallow. It helps you swallow.

The larynx does another special thing. *[Continue speaking as the child has hand on your throat.]* When I talk, you feel my larynx vibrate. And when I am quiet, you don't feel anything. Aren't you glad God gave you a larynx? If you had no larynx you would be able to move your mouth all you wanted to, but no voice would come out. Then you wouldn't be able to tell anybody if you were hungry or tired or cold.

Thank You, God, for creating my larynx and making me able to talk. Amen.

#175

Theme: Healthy Body

My Tongue

Materials: *lemon juice, syrup, salt water, fruit juice*

Jesus made your mouth special. It's what you use to eat food. He gave you teeth to help you chew. He gave you a tongue so you can taste things. Did you know that your tongue can tell you what you are eating, even if you can't see it with your eyes?

[Blindfold your child or have him/her close eyes. Have child dip finger in small samples of lemon juice, pancake syrup, water, water with salt dissolved in it, and one or two flavors of fruit juice, and touch it to his/her tongue.] As you taste each liquid,

tell me what your tongue tastes. Is it sweet? Is it salty? Is it sour? Your tongue can also taste things that are bitter and nasty. But I won't make you taste those! You don't have to taste bad things to know that Jesus made your tongue able to taste. Jesus made us so we can enjoy lots of things, but we don't have to do bad things to know that the good ones are good.

Thank You, Jesus, for making my tongue, and thank You for making me able to taste so I can enjoy my food. Amen.

Theme: Healthy Body

#176

Balance

Materials: *a glass of water*

Turn around and around as fast as you can—now stop. What happens? That's right—you feel dizzy! Do you know why you feel dizzy? Watch what happens to this cup of water. Let's swirl the water in the cup; then we'll stop and set it down. See how it takes a few seconds for the water to stop moving after we stop twirling it? The same thing happens to a little place inside your head—your inner ear. When you turn around and around, the fluid goes around and around. When you stop, it takes a few seconds for it to stop, just like the water in the cup.

Jesus made this place in your inner ear to help you keep your balance. This is the part in your body that helps you know if you are right side up or upside down. If you didn't have this special part, or if this part wasn't working right, you would fall down all the time. Wasn't Jesus wonderful to make that little place inside our inner ear so we can keep our balance? Jesus is wonderful!

Thank You, Jesus, for making me able to keep my balance. Amen.

#177

Theme: Healthy Body

Humidity

Materials: *mirror, paper towel*

Our bodies are mostly water, and they need water to live. We don't need water only in our food and to drink; we even need water in our air. Did you know there is water in the air you breathe? We can't see it, because it's in tiny drops. Let's do an experiment to collect some of it.

[Wipe the mirror with a paper towel. Have child hold the mirror in front of mouth but not touching it.] Now breathe out. *[Have child breathe in and out two or three times.]* Now look at the mirror. What do you see? It is water! There is water in the air that you breathe out. We call this water "vapor" because we can't see it, but we know it is there.

When Jesus made our world, He put water in the air so that we would have the right amount of water in the air to breathe. Animals need it too. Other places, such as the moon, don't have water in the air. We could not live there unless we took our own air with us and breathed through a mask.

Isn't Jesus wonderful? He thought of everything we'd need, even water in the air.

Thank You, Jesus, for making water in the air. Amen.

Theme: Nature

#178

My Heart

Your heart is a little pump, about the size of your fist. *[Have child make a fist.]* Your heart fits inside your chest. Its job is to pump the blood through your whole body. It pumps blood all the way up to your brain inside your head, and all the way down to your toes, so that every part of your body gets enough blood to make it grow and be healthy.

Put your hand on your chest. Do you feel a little *thump, thump, thump* in your chest? You are feeling your heart working! You can also feel the *thump, thump* when you feel a certain spot on your neck, or a certain spot on your wrist. *[Help child find pulse in his/her neck and wrist.]* Your heart is not in your neck or in your wrist—it's only in your chest. But every part of your body gets blood pumped to it by your heart, and that's why you can feel it even in other places.

Your heart works all the time, whether you're awake or asleep. When Jesus made your body, He thought of everything. I'm so glad Jesus made our hearts and made them work right.

Thank You, Jesus, for making my heart. Amen.

Theme: Healthy Body

My Backbone

Materials: *several spools of thread, a piece of string*

Jesus knew your back needed to be strong to hold the rest of your body up. So He made a backbone. But Jesus didn't put only one bone up your back. If He had, your back would have to stay perfectly straight all the time. You wouldn't be able to bend over and touch your toes. You wouldn't be able to bend over sideways or stretch. You would just have to be still.

[Help child thread cord through several spools. Tie a knot on each end. Then show how the column of spools can bend slightly from side to side, though it still stays some-

what upright and cannot be bent over in half.]

Your backbone is something like this. There are several little bones. We have a cord that runs up the middle called our spinal cord. It goes all the way to our head. *[Allow child to feel your backbone since it is difficult to feel one's own.]*

I'm so glad Jesus gave me a backbone so I can sit up or stand.

Thank You, Jesus, for making my backbone so I can stand up straight, and thank You for making it flexible so I can bend. You are wonderful! Amen.

Theme: Healthy Body

Devotion

#180